Master mode
BY
Angelo Aulisa

Angelo Aulisa

Master mode Table of contents

Angelo Aulisa

Introduction Master mode

Hi friends beloved friends , one new book on pure mysticism & physics , Master mode , is an incredible beautiful enchanting book the fifth essence of mysticism is really enclosed in it , millions cant by such a wisdom , is a unique eternal journey into the inner mystery reality of an organic unity that the meaning of mysticism inner sciences , you will go through the highest methodology of mysticism the most sophisticate exclusive methodology of meditation of Zen are enclosed into this treasure of book , factual scientific methodology for your day to day life useful factual , not esoteric at all , all the topics of the highest revelation of mysticism are clear spell describe into this short enchanting book , the elixir of mysticism is distillate here in this book the highest wisdom is impart in this book is the transmission of the lamp , that why the title Master mode is really the Master mode vision of life and death spell with such accuracy that you will be shock , if you really read meditative in Zen in meditation in love this book and understand the real meaning of what as being transmitted in wisdom you will get enlightened by simple reading this book , the impossible as been made possible in this book the transmission of the lamp of the master , Master mode is a divine sacred holy inner eternal journey , certain physics is spell accurate in this book physics means the science knowledge of nature , physics is the search research of understanding of the behavior of the universal body how it behave , and how the intrinsic law forces energy in motion into the universal body behave , the goal of physics is to understand the behavior of the universal body and is intrinsic law and finally define them know them , physics is not a rigid science it welcome all sciences such as astrology , astrophysics , quantum mathematics , all new avenue that bring understanding of the universal body are welcome and of course per excellence mysticism the inner science of the inner mystery reality of an organic unity which a human being his , physics welcome it as the human being is the most important expression of nature of existence of eternity itself , what emerge is a unique sciences that surpass all understanding of human kind up to now , an amazing beautiful book shocking for many verses , Master mode is an updating of all of my books a clarification the apex of all of my books , necessary to understand clear all other books 17 books that I have being writing in the last 8 years of my life , Master mode is the 18 book of my collection of jewels a diamond in all the sense category D the best quality of diamond , here in master mode mysticism is spelling like a song the divine melody his a divine sacred holy melody of mysticism of inner secrets revealed , it was necessary this updating of mysticism & physics it give a clarity to all of my other books I suggest to all humanity to read go through all my books but do not miss the Master mode is really a diamond of wisdom that as no equal and will have no equal for the next thousands of years , the best the highest wisdom of mysticism ever write in the history of all our so called civilization without any doubt , and it will remain so for the next thousands years trust , because I write books from my own experience of enlightenment I am even if you cannot say I am in enlightenment but we have to talk completely totally enlightened the master of all the masters ever happen the legal representative enlightened on this planet earth today , I live immerse into an oceanic light the oceanic light of the core and source of the mystery of the universal body and of life and death and of all duality of mind and dialectics , eternity itself meaning no begin no end oceanic light , hence the term enlightened enlightenment from the oceanic light of eternity itself is not casual , eternity as no size is just infinity the size of eternity vanish into an open relativity not absolute at all just an infinite opening into infinity , eternity is huger bigger above beyond transcendental than the universal body itself actually ultimate canvas reality where the mysterious sacred holy show of the universal body is display paint , eternity is infinite freedom from whole and everything time space duality of mind and dialectics , the real freedom , is infinite bliss sacred holy divine infinite silence peace rich with intrinsic subtle ecstasy zest, core and source of unconditional love intelligence , into eternity you in essence are at home enlightened , immortal resurrected already into the present life that you are living awake from unconscious asleep and various hypnosis , an organic unity clean of ego mind unconscious which is a huge task in essence is eternity itself , is an eternal journey the journey of your consciousness formless awareness that end nowhere ever , the form the body die but your inner essence in consciousness formless awareness are eternal immortal , mind you the resurrection is a conscious alchemy not gross not material not physical but a subtle mysterious alchemy conscious from unconscious to inner being witness consciousness universal consciousness to nothingness emptiness to non being body incorporeal where forms duality of mind time space completely annihilate into formless unfocused relation less awareness that is just an I am ness infinite light infinite relaxation ultimate essence into the core and source of eternity itself, where when you leave your body one day your essence, fragrance, quality, data of intelligence that you refine in thousands of life your DNA in short, annihilate diffuse dissolve into intrinsic to eternity for an eternal resurrection that the meaning of resurrection , a conscious mysterious subtle alchemy , in Master mode all of this inner mystery reality of mysticism are spell in accuracy and much more of course , I welcome all of you into this enchanting eternal inner journey , hope you delight rejoice enjoy , and have convergence of evolution of your DNA in intelligence an opening mutation of understanding , and certain an updating of consciousness awareness to our contemporary age 2019 , welcome thank you Angelo Aulisa

Master mode

BY

Angelo Aulisa

Friends beloved friends , they are two big news today one bad news and one good news , the good news is that they are no good news and the bad news is do not listen to the bad news , friends enough of propaganda dictatorial tyrant style like Mussolini use to do in the 1930 , we are not stupid basically they are no fake news around the world every network media news has an accurate filter censure for every news he deliver , the one who has invented the fake news is called Mustafa atlas Donald trump because he is a dictator a tyrant psycho that he do not want any criticism to his way of thinking , a real vicious game propaganda because you do not think like me so his fake news absurd only a dictator tyrant behave like this , but you have to know that critics criticism is sacred holy the world is what is today evolve intelligent only because of critics and criticism , critics trigger dialogue critics trigger creativity critics trigger growth opening , without critics we would have been at the stone age yet , because that what is really intelligence the quality of creating dialogue that modify change mutate the lie that Trump utter mercy less into truth , he lie in continuity constant because when you utter a lie you have to say thousands lie to cover up the single lie that you have utter , and all dialogue play become an absolute hypocrisy a false , so if you don't think like he think Trump you are telling fake news but this is pure dictator ship that tend to monopolize a single distort vision full of lie the vision of Trump for the entire world , we would never allowed this propaganda dictator style we will always and always assert the truth he may called it fake news because is a psycho but the reality is that the world is intelligent conscious aware and we cannot allowed the lies of Trump to be believed as truth , dear Trump you can full some people some time but you cannot full all the people all the time you can forget about we know who you are beyond the mask persona that you show to the world a real tyrant dictator psycho , what the news are doing is a sacred holy creative criticism that trigger dialogue growth opening, evolution intelligence the search for truth that what trigger criticism , we will never allowed you to monopolize the world with your lies neurosis narrow vision of nationalist fascist racist sectarian ideology of extreme right we will fight back forever with the truth authenticity in our hands be sure of it, yours is the worst type of propaganda for ignorant people we are not ignorant we like criticism and critics because this make the world evolve grow open in intelligence awareness and consciousness , . And also a culture a philosophy a religion or an ideology of far right as you have that is simple neurosis lies and insanity, and identification with collective unconscious and individual unconscious identification with tradition dead of the past out of date expire, however a culture a religion an extreme far right hallucination that do not allowed criticism is not worthy of been, is a fake extreme ideology a fake religion that is better to be done abolish band , because any true vision it welcome always and always any criticism and is ready to discuss to have a conversation about any new insight and about any modification that the critics propose if a vision is true it do not fear any criticism it welcome it all the time , instead a fake ideology as old out of date expire religions or culture or philosophy or your fake extreme ideology of far right idiom and idiom is one who live in is private dream not connected with reality, are always contrary against the critics because the critics it expose the lies the falsity the illiterate ignorance the neurosis of the fake vision that you have or they have religions society system culture , To all journalist critics is sacred holy divine never stop to do it is what make the world grow opening evolve expand explore new territory having breaking through convergence of evolution of the DNA of human being , this dictator who say if you do not think like me you are a terrorist or if you do not think like me are fake news are criminal they commit a crime against humanity against freedom against democracy against truth against love against peace against the very consciousness awareness of human being have to be brought in criminal court for crime against humanity , More to Macron we do not want any new army in Europe you have lost path way trek of civilization an ultimate state of civilization which means abolish band of all weapons deadly as nuclear hydrogen missile chemical biological weapons conventional weapons are a crime against humanity meant to kill destroy an extension of your own consciousness awareness sacred holy divine are device of death that the new world constitution as band abolish, the existing weapons have to be destroy deactivate and not allowed to build new one, are the worst crime against humanity and civilization and love and freedom, the factory who produce new weapons have to change their production into beneficial item for humanity or face criminal court for crime against humanity, as a consequence the army military will dissolve abolish finish, and as a consequence no more wars or bloodshed or destruction catastrophe horrible atrocity no more weapons no more military and no more wars because without weapons you cannot fight wars , what you have to do is to call table of peace of all the nations of the world and discuss have a conversation how to deactivate the exiting weapons and destroy them and how to transform the factory that produce device of death called weapons into beneficial item for humanity this the direction orientation of civilization , an ultimate state of civilization urgent needed , call conference table of peace for all world and discuss the issue the matter urgent , the new army for Europe that you propose is a megalomaniac idea come back to your sense , we the Italian we are not going to pay not even an euro for this childish infantile megalomaniac idea , because you have lost direction orientation of civilization a real ultimate state of civilization that the all humanity dream since ten thousand years a world without weapons military and wars, that are bloodshed killing and destruction, like you celebrate yesterday in millions of millions of sacred holy human being enough of wars military and weapons come back to your sense and work for peace freedom democracy meritocracy, love intelligence, consciousness awareness , we the Italian do not pay a euro for this megalomaniac idea we have to build restore our nation, we have project more important as supporting the poverty in Italy an make the infrastructure , of our nation new that are falling apart on our citizen that is it ....Angelo Aulisa

Angelo Aulisa

Chapter 2 Secularism, tradition, ideology Master mode

Hi friends beloved friends, a new book the master, a new adventure begin, unfortunate the subjects are hard subjects so it begin with an up heel task, the world is evolving, mutating, changing, towards freedom, democracy in the sense of human right freedom, towards meritocracy a better quality of living better shaping of living, technology is changing mutating the face of the objective world rapidly , our contemporary age is an age of changing fast, mutating fast towards new wave of living in freedom in quality of living always better in intelligence ,better shape, our DNA is evolving mutating fast either individual DNA either collective DNA of all humanity is having convergence of evolution breaking through amazing beautiful in synchronicity with our individual DNA overlapping with it, consciousness too is in a process of refinement evolving mutating rapidly higher and higher , consciousness & DNA are overlapping each other in process of evolution they are refining simultaneous and together , because at first the evolution happen into the DNA simultaneous in synchronicity also consciousness refine itself into higher refine sensitiveness into light consciousness more and more , and cannot be otherwise if the process of evolution of your DNA is stark also your consciousness is stark they intersect each other indivisible , cannot be a refine consciousness without having going through a refinement of DNA simple impossible , is an individual process intimate they are mystics that through meditation have refine their DNA and consequence their consciousness, and they are individual that have refine just their DNA without knowing anything of meditation they lark behind , and they are ordinary people who have not develop either their DNA or either their consciousness they lark really behind they are asleep unconscious walking in a sleep , so they are different stage level of people around the world , but basically I repeat DNA & consciousness intersect mingled each other and they evolve grow opening in synchronicity never otherwise , we are living in an age contemporary as never before the world as witness, full of freedom opening the world today is a small global village , never before the human being as had the possibility to travel move from one plays to another of the world in hours , the web the internet the news media network they give simultaneous information in real time from everywhere around the world and even our solar system is monitored quite accurate , even if our solar system is just a dot into the infinite universe , but however we are living an age very free open full of possibility and potentiality as never before has this humanity, we are lucky . Anyhow this are the possibility what could be possible, unfortunate the situation of the world is chaotic they are part of the world that are living thousands of years back ward due the secularism of their culture religions that do not allowed any evolution in intelligence in consciousness in formless awareness opening , or any true authentic living contemporary to our age , because basically they are totally identify with their collective unconscious where they are store all the traditions dead and expire, all the ideology of their religion dogma pseudo believe superstition prejudice , infantile credo believe , lies , falsity neurosis , and the identification is so complete total the hypnosis as gone so deep, that they live no window for new understand new approach new opening that the intelligence of the world as brought about in light to the world in thousands of years of evolution in all the field, literature, psychology, sciences, physics, mysticism, arts , alchemist etc.. , they live no space for freedom for meritocracy, democracy human right evolution of intelligence , and they live in a kind of obscurantism secularism in darkness, identify with the darkness of the collective unconscious consequence identify with the individual unconscious that is a consequence of living in the darkness of the collective unconscious in absolute illiterate ignorance , large part of the world they live a primitive age, of thousands of years ago a secularism stench an obscurantism , that create a big gap with the rest of the world that is heading fast towards the future of physics & mysticism and they lark far behind , going in such part of the world where the secularism of religions out of date expire, infantile childish, superstition, prejudice, illiterate ignorance is their reality, is like coming back thousands of years into the past, and is very dangerous to go in such a plays of the world , because there is a big contrast of vision of living a big gap of thousands of years , in this part of the world life as stop evolving growing mutating , at thousands of years ago at when their prophet their masters dies and all the population society of this part of the world dies with when their masters , they live castrate for any conscious evolution , that has never stop evolving, growing, changing, mutating , opening, creating a split second , consciousness fundamental law intrinsic to the universal body that is a pulsation of love a pulsation of intelligence a pulsation of light wave a pulsation of dharma quality such as bliss sacred holy such as peace silence rich with intrinsic ecstasy such as playfulness celebration such as freedom the very ground essence of consciousness , a pulsation of creativity that has never stop pulsating for a split second since the big bang event when consciousness it come into light in relation to the universal body itself , and in this part of the world where exist this obscurantism secularism that their religions culture philosophy are, they live a very abstract reality backwards of thousands of years, stench with dead traditions that they cherish in very infantile, childish retarded illiterate ignorant way , this gap of age of contemporary is very dangerous ,they can hinder the process of civilization and evolution in intelligence consciousness awareness of the world for hundreds of years is better carefully to avoid to go in such part of the world because they are fanatics, hypnotize identify with past dead out date expire traditions, is like they have stop the evolution opening of intelligence the growth the opening in freedom, they have stop life to flow and all and everything is dead repress conditioning with the most ugly traditions, traditional behavior coming from their identification with the darkness of collective unconscious and individual unconscious as a consequence, traditions is not Zen at all, as you may know the unconscious is the foundation of your life house, the unconscious as deep roots into your neurons whatever as being projected feed into your neurons since early age constitute make up is the unconscious , functioning in a chain reaction into your brain the neurons are vector of thought believe emotion and they move fast in a chain reaction into your brain in you , conditioning your life with contents that your neurons have been feed basically conditioning wounds of tradition repression of freedom falsity lies neurosis superstition prejudice , your unconscious is nine tenth of your life like an iceberg nine tenth is under water one tenth surface up to the water that one tenth is the thin conscious that you show live in your day to day life , but any new situation which goes against your conditioning contents that has been projected feed into your neurons, and the nine tenth of your unconscious bubble up with ferocious revenge in a rage violent , the unconscious is very powerful irrational knows only need is wild ferocious barbarous a tragedy   . The situation is dramatic the gap of contemporary from one plays of the world to another is so huge of thousands of years , the fragmentation of different culture religions philosophy are so many hundreds of different morality culture traditions , the world is like a broken mirror in hundreds of pieces and each piece reclaim that is the truth, bullshit sorry, the truth is the empty mirror whole and some , no labels no adjectives no contents that what is an empty consciousness an empty mirror whole and some , and each of this sectarian fragmentation into out of date expire religions extreme ideology extreme traditions out of date expire, create great division split into humanity ,& consequence of fearless wars, catastrophe bloodshed, horrible atrocity killing destruction , into my understand this heritage of obscurantism secularism of culture of dead traditions of the past, out of date religions of the ancient past, that are really a nightmare of neurosis lies falsity have to be abolish band they have peacefully give up resignation , for give way to the truth authenticity of an empty consciousness fundamental intrinsic law of the universal body pulsation of creativity pulsation of quality love intelligence , label less content less adjectives less neutral to gender color race age , one consciousness for the entire universal body all forms of it and living being of it one consciousness for the entire planet earth and forms of it and living being of it , on the surface we are 8 billion different forms, in the within an unique oceanic consciousness extension of one another holy sacred divine , that do not create any division split into humanity anymore , but unite humanity put together humanity into an organism into an harmony into a mystical union of love peace , bliss , playfulness, celebration affirmation of life in all of is sacred holy aspect faces of life in freedom , this new dawn of consciousness formless awareness is urgent needed for the entire world to eradicate the obscurantism of secularism , of ideology traditions ,all ideology traditions extreme and non-extreme are dangerous, noble ideology included the nation, the flag, nationalism , the false religions, the family the society, the system, are bogus division they create division split into humanity consequence antagonism fearless wars, killing destruction bloodshed, for futile motivation of ideals, traditions expire out of date fanatics , my understand is no ideology just nothingness emptiness universal light consciousness, content less adjectives less label less, neutral to gender color race age, neutral to any interpretation of the little unconscious men, consciousness is to infinite to enclose in labels contents of part or partial adjectives , consciousness is everywhere & nowhere in particular expand intrinsic to the universal body fundamental intrinsic law of the universal body like an inner tread that runs through all forms and living being of the universal body , it belong to itself is nobody monopoly , a pulsation of light wave of love of intelligence a pulsation of quality creativity and anyone can be one in mystical union with consciousness the path the way meditation , silence love , dancing , singing , painting playing music , sculpting running or any activity that take you into no mind into your inner being is meditation that link connected you in mystical union sacred holy divine with universal consciousness. However we need urgent to widespread this wisdom this knowledge this new dawn of civilization of consciousness of formless awareness, the huge gap of contemporary, that the obscurantism of secularism of traditional behavior of unconscious behavior create is dangerous many wars are active for futile motivation of ideals many bloodshed catastrophe horrible atrocity, and basically is very dangerous already to go in place nations where the obscurantism of secularism is there idiom reality , idiom is a Greek word that means one who live in is private dream not connected relate to the reality and the people who live in a idiom are called idiot ,it create fanaticism illiterate ignorance , MS multiple sclerosis , Alzheimer losing of capability of brain dislocation one do not know where it is anymore a very terrible disease, the cause of it the bogus foundation of your life the conditioning contents projected feed into your neurons that make up your unconscious , & the house your life around 40 years collapsed, and the tragedy of psychological diseases, dozens of neurosis erupted , humanity need urgent a quantum leap into DNA evolution into consciousness into formless awareness , you have to know that when you do not allowed a convergence of evolution of your DNA the cells that were ready to evolve shrink back and die, and the consequence are dramatic cancer is the outcome of the missing evolution of your DNA , because you repress naturalness freedom spontaneity you repress your DNA and consequence your inner being and consciousness a catastrophe is the outcome, like cancer and multiple psychological diseases ask the psychologist they all will agree with my . Anyhow this fragmentation of the world into traditions dead out of date expire and traditional unconscious behavior, into hundreds of different ideology extreme and non & consequence ideological unconscious behavior, create the obscurantism called secularism of past ancient out of date expire religions , and the outcome is a very diseases human being conscious retarded crippled , with inferiority complex and guilty complex , is dramatic , my proposal to having a convergence of evolution a quantum leap irrational jump into our contemporary age 2019 a new dawn of civilization, meditation consciousness, formless awareness , were men will face the sunrise of consciousness alone without any mediator of false hypothetical superstition prejudice religions, or fake priest that they do not know even the abc of consciousness, but what they know is repeating parrot like out of date expire ancient book that are a nightmare of neurosis lies , the new men will face alone the new dawn of consciousness in silence in love in meditation, dancing, celebrating in playfulness, singing, painting , running he will rejoice the new era of consciousness awareness , the answer is always a world humanity conscious aware awake, from unconscious asleep and various hypnosis, this body the consciousness awareness this planet the lotus paradise for a new era of harmony civilization ultimate civilization to unfold happen, with no weapons no wars no military no bloodshed no killing no destruction no catastrophe horrible atrocity , the first step of civilization is no weapons abolish band no wars no military until when this happen civilization will be just a beautiful dream talking but never ever as happen , because basically all of this crime and crime against humanity that weapons are wars are military are criminal are is all coming from the unconscious staff of human being , once the unconscious is clear overcome erase, and the path way is inner journey meditation inner being witness consciousness, inner consciousness formless awareness, the witness consciousness is the medicine the fire that evaporate burn the wounds conditioning of the unconscious and the cosmos reabsorb them, they are no tablet or medicine for the free clear the unconscious the medicine is the witness consciousness that is at a certain distance from body mind ego unconscious complex the witness consciousness encompass your organic unity aloof at a certain distance that why you can see your thought emotion mind body ,, all of this nightmare of crime of humanity will disappear dissolve vanish , a world conscious aware awake to the witness consciousness is the only answer always and always ......Angelo Aulisa

Angelo Aulisa

Chapter 3 Elixir of mysticism Master mode

Friends beloved friends , ordinary people this humanity lives in the dimension of having , horizontal linear logic , Aristotelian rational association of thought that means a double fold logic yes or no , black or white , from abc, to xvz , on the surface of objectivity a material dimension of matter , at infinite regression , the dimension of having tomorrow is gone be the real thing the happiness the love the loving attitude not today , gazing starring at the horizon and the horizon is receding backwards each second all the time the more you gaze star at it the more recede it remain always at the horizon and tomorrow never come , because the past tense is dead and the present of ordinary people is a projection of the past into present a disease present loaded with past conditioning traditions and the future the horizon as yet to come is just imagination and existence as no obligation to fulfill your expectation instead existence the whole been absolutely irrational it never categorically fulfill your expectation , but it goes on natural spontaneous irrational each moment it remain always a suffuse mystery and that the beauty of life of the whole existence that it remain always an unknown mystery in spite of your planning programming , sometime many time it may happen as you plane programmed but then is just a superficial ego mind unconscious happening , on the surface , on the dimension of having material , life thanks to the whole existence remain always a suffuse mystery unknown each moment an exploration fresh new each split second irrational and that the beauty , in spite of your afford of programming planning that is an afford to make life dead and dull , when you know already what you are going to do today tomorrow the day after tomorrow programmed planed you have kill the mystery the beauty of the unknown moment to moment flowing of the present and life , and life become boring a terrible annoyed , like you say let go and see the sunrise and your friend say but I have already seen the sunrise what is there , but a sunrise is never the same it may be clouds painting the sun with incredible design it may be clear sky and the sun look like just like an apple red orange huge big beautiful and fresh breeze blowing early morning , each moment new fresh unknown mysterious that the beauty of life and death too let me say , the unknowability , that remain a mystery always , and remember the mystery is that which as no cause is called mystery that which as a cause your mind ego unconscious programming planning is not a mystery as a cause your mind ego and cannot be big that your mind ego is just ordinary superficial living boring a mortal annoyance , life is beautiful in a present less present in the moment flowing fresh each moment unknown unplanned not programmed , then ha this the ha experience describe by the psychologist each second new ha this thousand time this at a stage that when you look at a trees you do not know that is green or when you look at the sky you do not know that is blue is just treeing is just sky ing is just a river rive ring is just the mystery of consciousness life flowing in a kind of newness now ness then you are in for the greatest surprise of your life it become a miracle of playfulness sacred holy a miracle of celebration and most of all you are never boring annoyed but fresh in the moment into a present less present intrinsic to the mystery miracle that life is , by this I am not saying throw away your passport no they are objective things to take care but just factual memory is enough to do it , however tomorrow never come in the horizontal dimension the happiness the love the loving approach remain always at the horizon what come is always today now here the moment , tomorrow death come finally because death is the only unchanging reality all the rest in life is a constant changing mutating each second changing on the surface of life is the only truth reality . Anyhow into the moment into a present less present open a gate less gate of the vertical dimension the dimension of being , of deeper and higher you close your eyes be into the present moment look within inwards bring the attention within you, into the present less present that as no relation with past or future because are dead tense, the moment the present is the gate less gate to your inner journey into your inner being is the dimension of deeper and higher , you let go within the so called dark matter or gravitational energy field will bent pull your light consciousness deep within your inner being , at the deepest point of your inner being when you are relax centered you will realize rediscover that you are not your body, not your emotional layer not your mind not your thought process not your unconscious staff conditioning wounds ,not even your senses, but you are a crystal clear witness consciousness that witness all and everything layer aspect of your organic unity and you will realize rediscover that you are simple a mirror like quality an empty mirror that reflect all and everything that surround you any situation circumstance in the moment and next moment the empty mirror is empty again ready to reflect what is coming next situation circumstance , this are the chief quality of your inner being, witness consciousness that encompass spherical your organic unity at a certain distance aloof, that is why you can see your body your thought your emotion your unconscious staff conditioning wounds , and mirror like quality an empty mirror that what is your inner being , this is not coolness but the simple nature of the whole existence , however deeper and deeper into meditation your witness consciousness will witness all the clouds that are passing by your inner sky clouds of thought are rushing like a river flowing down heels , clouds of unconscious staff conditioning wounds that are dark clouds heavy clouds difficult to watch to witness , witness read clouds of emotion that have roots into your hearth the read clouds of emotion are more difficult to witness and be detached because they have deeper roots in your emotional layer but neither the less elusive , emotion are not real love but emotion are elusive as the thought are elusive they pass and go and disappear , and on and on deep into meditation your witness consciousness will witness all the process of your organic unity , a moment come of gap between one thought and another a moment come of gap between one emotion and another a moment come when your unconscious conditioning and wounds are less strong and gap happen into your unconscious too gap of emptiness nothingness , the moment of gap are the moment when your inner sky start to shine with blueness no clouds they have pass and go they will come back, but in meditation the moment of gap of blue sky those are the moment of meditation for the first time emptiness nothingness silence , the gap in between is the real moments of meditation, let go easy deep into the gap expand it they have to become the full inner sky blue, when at the deepest point of your inner being there is only a huge gap silence emptiness nothingness and the inner sky is shining blue without clouds that is it you are centered deep into your inner being , and the witness consciousness having nothing else to witness it turn up on itself and it twisted become turn into pin drop silence gate less gate to your inner universal consciousness , and here at this stage happen an annihilation of your inner being into universal consciousness your inner being twisted into universal consciousness and the size change into universal body size is a break through sacred holy divine majestic , and your witness consciousness turn into twisted into witnessing consciousness of the whole universal body , at this point your inner being is the whole universal body and the whole universal consciousness you in essence are intrinsic into the whole universal consciousness and body huge and big as the universal body is big and huge , you flow intrinsic into universal consciousness and you are everywhere and nowhere in particular expand into the whole universal body and forms and living being of it , and rising higher and higher the process of rising higher and higher is trigger by the so called dark energy or expansive energy field that will rise higher and higher your light consciousness at the event of the universal body itself expanding in synchronicity with the expansion of the universal body itself that is expanding each split second at incredible speed due the pulling higher of the expansive energy field called dark energy , you flow move expand in essence intrinsic to the expansion of the universal body an infinite opening of your light empty consciousness and rise higher and higher trigger by the expansive energy field called dark energy that pull your light consciousness higher and higher at infinity , deeper on into meditation and the so called dark flux or flowing energy field that move flows planet stars galaxies in and out of the event of the universal body itself will move and flows circulate also your light empty consciousness in and out of the event of the universal body like an universal breath, the universal body breath in and out, into the overlapping non being body incorporeal and in an irrational eternal flow move breath your light consciousness will move circulate flow in and out of the universal body into the overlapping non being body incorporeal, is a sacred holy divine stage of your inner journey into meditation majestic , the event boundary of the universal body are annihilating disappearing into the overlapping nonbeing body incorporeal , then nothingness emptiness the witnessing consciousness is turning up on itself because into non being body incorporeal forms time space duality are annihilate completely , and the witnessing consciousness turn up on itself because as no more relation to be , because consciousness is always in relation to a subject or object until the boundary event of the universal body consciousness his in relation of the universal body itself is huge infinite , but at the event of it at the boundary of it where is annihilating into non being body incorporeal it turn up on itself no more subject or object it ceases to be or better it twisted turn into formless relation less unfocused awareness that is just an I am ness , infinite light infinite relaxation expand everywhere and nowhere in particular intrinsic to non being body incorporeal that is infinite relaxation ha this   , awareness ultimate essence into the core and source of the mystery of the universal body and of life and death and of all duality of mind eternity itself that means no begin no end infinite oceanic light that what is eternity no size it vanish into an infinite open relativity not absolute at all because has no begin or end it vanish into infinity as the last equation of quantum mathematics and no more equation infinity is the dead end of quantum mathematics , eternity is huger bigger , beyond above transcendental to the universal body itself, eternity is the ultimate canvas reality where the mysterious sacred holy show of the universal body is paint display , here into eternity you in essence are at home enlightened awake immortal resurrected already , awake from unconscious sleep forever awake from various hypnosis forever , eternity is infinite freedom from whole and everything forms time space duality the real freedom Moksha , is infinite bliss sacred holy divine is infinite silence peace rich with intrinsic subtle ecstasy , eternity is the core and source of unconditional love core and source of intelligence, that intelligence is nothing else but the essence quality data of intelligence fragrance of thousands of enlightened one that have annihilate into eternity for an eternal resurrection, the key that connected link you in mystical union with the essence quality of the whole resurrected enlightened one is love , for example you love your Jesus you can have a date with Jesus and share wisdom essence quality be with him for while that refresh regenerate you so much, or any enlightened that you love they are hundreds of thousands that have had an eternal resurrection , when I say this to my mother she start to laugh and I tell her you love your Jesus she was silent a moment then she say yes of course , then I say to her I will arrange a meeting then is ok she laugh loud content , the resurrection immortality is not a joke but a true authentic reality, where do you think that the enlightened one goes , they annihilate dissolve into the core and source of eternity their quality essence data of intelligence fragrance are intrinsic to eternity itself in mystical union sacred holy divine , you can be one in mystical union with any of the enlightened one that you have loved or love into formless awareness into light consciousness , when an enlightened one leave the body is a fresh new begin he annihilate formless into an universal body intrinsic into universal consciousness flowing intrinsic to whole universal body forms of it living being of it , stars planets galaxies , sky , wind, ear , oceans , living being , rocks , nature , animals , you in essence into consciousness will be everywhere and nowhere in particular expand into intrinsic to all universal body , you will be roses and the fragrance of roses and when you smell the fragrance of roses in a split second you have smell the whole eternity , the resurrection is a conscious alchemy not gross not material not physical but a conscious alchemy from unconscious to inner being to witness consciousness to inner consciousness to nothingness emptiness gate less gate to non being body incorporeal where time space forms duality of mind annihilate completely into formless awareness I am ness infinite light infinite relaxation into the core and source of eternity that begin less endless oceanic light, hence the term enlightenment enlightened from the infinite light of eternity is not casual , the resurrection immortality is a true authentic reality for those who refine is light consciousness completely totally into light , is a mysterious subtle alchemy the resurrection , for those who have a little hard skull and remain unconscious , reincarnation at the moment they leave the body a reincarnation is generate and a journey into the cosmic unconscious, to come back soon into play into another form of body , they have not learned the lesson the joke that life is they need a little more time, existence will go on give as many opportunity you need as many reincarnation you need until when then you got the joke the lesson that life is and you got enlightened awake from unconscious asleep and various hypnosis , life is an eternal journey that end nowhere your consciousness awareness are eternal immortal, until a final eternal resurrection then you will have no more reincarnation no more body , and you will be intrinsic one in mystical union with eternity itself , an organic unity clean of unconscious ego mind in essence is eternity itself enlightened awake already resurrected forever and ever , death do not exist the form the body die but your consciousness awareness is an eternal journey endless , when your light consciousness is completely refine one return at home into eternity into a circle of zero the inner journey is from eternity unconscious to eternity totally conscious your light consciousness as refine completely itself as accomplish the aspiration of the whole existence and it return in a circle of zero at home into the core and source of eternity, that is oceanic light an alchemy dialectic of different law that the final synthesis is oceanic light that what it is eternity , the inner journey is from here to here where do you think to go always here and here ……flowing in freedom … formless into consciousness awareness into the core and source of the mystery of the universal body and of life and death and of all duality eternity itself the law of eternity ……..welcome Angelo Aulisa

Chapter 4 Religious freedom & God fiction Master mode

Friends beloved friends , this book is gone be a master piece in all the sense unfortunate they are subject that are a very hard up heel task hard subject , but the truth the opening evolution of human kind has to go through this stage of convergence of evolution mutation changing of individual DNA and collective DNA yes a new assertion as there is the collective unconscious and individual unconscious in the same there is individual and collective DNA and they evolve they opening towards freedom towards accomplish refining itself in synchronicity simultaneous ,and of course the DNA is overlapping with your own inner being and witness consciousness and universal consciousness, and if you allowed me to say there is also an universal DNA that what physics the science of nature, the academic science of studying search research of the behavior of the universal body and of all of is intrinsic law forces energy in motion intrinsic into the universal body , the goal of physics is to understand the behavior of the universal body and the behavior of all of the intrinsic law forces energy in motion intrinsic to the universal body, and finally know them define them , the strings theory of all whole and everything is an afford to know define the universal DNA of the universal body, so there is also an universal DNA , the material part of the universal body that you see is only 4 per cent, a pale shadow of an invisible intrinsic reality order hide to human eyes that is 96 per cent , and sure enough is a long work to understand know define the hide order of 96 per cent, but physics is on the way the path and working hard to do it physics is not a rigid science it welcome different fields of sciences such as astrophysics, quantum mathematics , astrology , and many other sciences intersect mingled merge with physics it uses all avenue and per excellence physics it welcome in in itself Mysticism that is the inner science of study search research of the inner reality mystery of an organic unity done with scientific methodology such as meditation, silence, love , painting , dancing , sculpting , acting , singing , playing music , running , tennis , or any activity that take you into no mind, into your inner being, into the present moment, into witness consciousness is meditation, any activity that do not interfere with the physical body the freedom of psychology of other individual of course, is meditation , and bridge link that connected the individual inner being (soul) from the known to the unknown of into universal consciousness in mystical union in oneness with universal consciousness that is a fundamental law intrinsic to the universal body, expand everywhere and nowhere in particular intrinsic to the universal body like a thread that runs through all forms and living being of the universal body, that is a pulsation of love a pulsation of intelligence a pulsation of light wave a pulsation of dharma quality such as bliss sacred holy divine , silence peace rich with intrinsic subtle ecstasy zest , playfulness , celebration , freedom the very ground essence of consciousness , a pulsation of affirmation of life in all of his face aspect in freedom sacred holy divine , consciousness is a pulsation of creativity that has never stop a split second pulsating since the event of big bang when it come into light into be in relation of the universal body itself onwards , and mediation is not contemplation is not concentration is not reflecting , is wrong associate the term word meditation is a wrong translation meditation, because the word carry wrong association that is not , to call it ZEN is better because no wrong association are carry by the term Zen no contemplation no concentration no reflection , on any subject or object Zen is subject less object less , just no mind all inclusive a stage of complete relaxation that include whole and everything, for example is half hours that I am writing this chapter and there is a bird a cuckoo that singing loud constant beautiful mysterious to me this singing cuckoo, is sacred divine music I include this singing divine music in my Zen ecstatic is a bliss , and if when you meditate you do not include the singing cuckoo then yours is not meditation , but concentration narrowing of the mind very cheap concentration , Zen meditation is a state all inclusive a stage of complete relaxation let go into your inner being witness consciousness and inner consciousness , no mind , a bliss divine sacred ecstatic , and the cuckoo is going on singing and other birds too incredible in the middle of new York where I am I have find a room where in the morning many birds are singing beautiful mysterious music I love it , however that what mysticism his and physics it welcome embrace mysticism because the study search inner and outer of an organic unity is fundamental because what of more important there is in nature of a human being , nothing, an organic unity per excellence is the focused attention of physics too and it uses welcome mysticism for this academic study research . However on and on on Zen deeper in meditation, universal consciousness, emptiness nothingness, are the gate less gate that annihilate your essence witnessing consciousness into non being body incorporeal where forms duality of mind , time space, completely annihilate , now for instance I want say that the teaching of Gautama the Buddha end here is Nirvana is just emptiness nothingness he did not added anything else to emptiness nothingness , I do not know why maybe for fear of creating a new ego or because he did not reach higher than this emptiness nothingness most probable , anyhow I go further emptiness is not just emptiness it as his opposite complementary into wholeness fullness , micro thesis macro antithesis friction of those and synthesis of big bang a whole universal body is create by such a friction, or synthesis of the law of eternity oceanic light , emptiness is not just a negative void empty at the same time as opposite complementary of wholeness fullness, that why Gautama the Buddha he did not conquer the all world because a negative emptiness void scare people , the renunciation is bogus useless sad masochist attitude, why renounce life sacred holy divine , if is just a dream why be scare of a dream is harmless you should celebrate rejoice in life is the greatest gift miracle of existence, the renunciation is coming from the Indian tradition of Maya all is an illusion Gautama was an Indian after all, an out shot of Indus, but I always say this equation to the Indus philosopher of Maya , mind ego unconscious plus reality existence equal to Maya illusion, because the reality the existence has no obligation to follow your collective an individual unconscious your mind ego unconscious at all, reality existence unfold happen in the present moment no past no future is a flowing moment by moment in consciousness into a present less now ness, existence as no obligation to fulfill your ego unconscious mind that live in the past in the future that are dead tense, that why to the Indus look like all an illusion , instead my equation is reality existence minus the mind ego unconscious equal to real authentic true life you flow in the moment in the present with existence, no unconscious request no mind request no ego request just here now flowing in consciousness moment by moment and whole and everything is authentic real true, holy sacred divine , minus mind minus ego minus unconscious and an organic unity in essence is eternity itself ,the discrimination of woman is a crime against humanity, if one as to seek search work hard methodology of meditation to finally come to a bare emptiness nothingness it look like useless and scare too, for the ordinary little unconscious men , in fact in India his vision did not take over to bare just emptiness void it look negative, void emptiness the core and source of whole existence , and the Indian mind is very colorful they did not digest it , they give meaning to whole and everything and Gautama the Buddha in India he did not appeal he take over in east Asia because they modify a little the vision of emptiness nothingness from the original vision of Gautama in India , also because Indian have a few philosophy already of emptiness , but in the same way just emptiness negative void nothingness, which for the Indian it look to bare that whole and everything come born out of that negative emptiness nothingness , and they never elaborate such a philosophy of emptiness they were simple forget , humanity as come across few time real authentic true approach vision of truth to reality but if you do not pay attention give relevance they are simple forget, the Indian are very colorful for them Brahman the God of creation is the source and core of whole existence anthropomorphic, childish infantile, but in line with the Indian mind , however Manik went up to the button of it the full circle cycle of zero, also because Manik is a contemporary mystic and has all the tools of mysticism, physics , psychology , literature etc.. and he elaborate it through experiencing it experimenting it in meditation in Zen for many years , and of course he reach higher of them all into the very core and source of the mystery of the universal body and of life and death and of all duality of mind and of all duality of dialectics , eternity itself no begin no end oceanic light , probable the master key of Manik is the fundamental law of eternity itself the law of nature the law of dialectics, of opposite complementary thesis , antithesis friction of those and synthesis, that again at his own turn become a new thesis and so on so forth , Manik defeat them all is the master of all the masters ever exist the legal representative on planet earth yahoo ha ha , anyhow let go on , the witnessing consciousness having no more relation of subject or object because consciousness is always and always in relation to a subject or object and into non being body whole annihilate time , space , forms , duality of mind , nothing survive into non being body incorporeal , turn up on itself and annihilate twisted into formless relation less unfocused awareness that is just an I am ness infinite light , infinite relaxation into the core and source of the mystery of the universal body and of life and death and of all duality of mind eternity itself meaning no begin no end eternity is infinite oceanic light , no size the size vanish into infinity as the last equation of quantum mathematics and no further equation follow in quantum mathematics infinity is the dead end the last equation of quantum mathematics , the size it vanish into an open relativity not absolute at all because no begin or end is just an infinite opening button less an abyss , eternity is huger bigger above beyond above transcendental, to the universal body itself actually the ultimate canvas reality where the mysterious sacred holy show of the universal body is display paint , eternity is infinite freedom from whole and everything time space forms duality of mind , the real freedom , and is infinite silence infinite peace and source and core of unconditional love and intelligence , an oceanic light hence the term enlightened , enlightenment , from the light of eternity , whiteness transparency , refreshing regenerating rejuvenating , and healing source it heal completely all of your organic unity and organs , for example I am 50 of age but I look like 30 , is the 25 years of meditation that I have being doing for real and been vegetarian the rejuvenating elixir , actually your body as an age but into consciousness formless awareness you have no age at all you are eternal always fresh in the split moment no age like the dew drop on the petal of roses early morning fresh that they shine like diamond , you have to know that the 80 years of life that you live into timeless space less eternity is just the blink of the eyes an you are gone nothing at all , and an organic unity a human being clean of unconscious ego mind that is a huge task , in essence is eternity itself enlightened immortal already resurrected , awake from unconscious asleep and various hypnosis , into eternity at home reside happen unfold the immortality & resurrection the resurrection is the most important item , you know if in this existence do not exist death and life was eternal all religions lose all appeal meaning, they could should give resignation right now nobody would be interest in religions try to think if death do not exist and life was eternal nobody would be interest in religions, if religions exist is only because we die the body die the form die and the mystery that as no cause why we die it as no cause, hence the mystery what has no cause create the mystery, what as cause is not a mystery but a cause and effect happen , so religions exist because of death hence that why the resurrection is the most important item , we want know the organic unity human being want know what happen after death, the resurrection is basically important is the greatest mystery of whole existence , the reason why all false out of date expire religions exist ,they play on this fear that human being has of death to dominate you, and all of them categorically give a laugh stock explanation of what resurrection his , it do not exist any paradise or hell they are device of religions to dominate you fearful human being they make you scare of hell and they make you greedy for paradise, both of them hypothetical they do not exist where it is for instance the geographic location , up on a clouds playing an harp or a flute all day long eternally try to think what a boredom , and how is it if a man die at 85 or 90 , with multiple sclerosis and Alzheimer the body completely dilapidate , what is gone do up on the clouds in paradise playing the harp or the flute trembling , so is better to die early , you reach the pearly gate at San Peter more young fresh , no my friends they are wish fulfilment of the little unconscious men , what you do not got here on earth you will got in paradise , in the middle east their Firdausi have rivers of wine in fact here they cannot have and they have boys always aging 16 in fact here in the middle east the homosexual they kill but in Firdausi they can have as much they want , the Indus paradise is ear condition paradise always cool in fact here they die of heat , and so on so forth the paradise of religions are a laughing stock hypothetical wish fulfilment of what you do not got here, they do not exist at all and so hell they scare you for dominate you with fear and greediness , in fact go and dig the grave in the graveyard cemetery and you will find all body in putrefaction eat by worm and rats , no there resurrection is a laughing stock a big lie a turning around humanity like puppet ,the resurrection is a conscious alchemy not gross not material not physical but a conscious alchemy subtle mysterious from unconscious when your consciousness originate from eternity itself to inner being to witness consciousness to universal consciousness to nothingness emptiness gate less gate to non being body incorporeal where forms , duality of mind , time space completely annihilate, into formless relation less unfocused awareness that is just I am ness infinite light infinite relaxation , awareness ultimate essence of the core and source of eternity itself transcendental above beyond life and death and of all duality of mind just eternal life, eternity where the dialectics of opposite complementary thesis antithesis friction and synthesis ceases and only eternal life , where one day when you leave your body your consciousness completely refine into light consciousness annihilate dissolve diffuse , your essence fragrance quality , data of intelligence that you have refine in thousands of life in short your DNA annihilate into eternity itself , into formless awareness reside unfold all the essence fragrance quality data of intelligence DNA , of all the enlightened one that have had an eternal resurrection, and the bridge link key to recall such essence quality data of intelligence DNA fragrance is your love for the one you do , when you leave the body is a new begin into eternity itself into formless awareness a new begin with an universal body of course formless in essence , you will flow intrinsic to universal consciousness intrinsic to all forms and living being of the universal body you will be everywhere and nowhere in particular intrinsic to the universal body and universal consciousness, you will be the core and source of it universal consciousness diffuse annihilate into planets galaxies stars , sky , wind , ear , space , time , oceans , intrinsic to all forms and living being of the universal body , intrinsic to nature , animals , flowers roses , you will be the fragrance of roses and when we smell the fragrance of roses in a split second you have smell the whole eternity , you in essence will be eternally from one universal body cycle into another universal body cycle eternally , your consciousness awareness is an eternal journey that end nowhere ever , the resurrection has happen unfold done, is like when in a room there is thousand light on and you added another lamp light what is gone do it only intensify the light already above in the room without disturbing the light already there above the room , eternity is oceanic light your light consciousness when annihilate into it only intensify the oceanic light of eternity without disturbing the oceanic light that already exist into it , the resurrection is a subtle mysterious alchemy , you return at home into eternity like a circle of zero the eternal journey is from eternity unconscious to eternity your light consciousness totally refine return at home into eternity, is an eternal journey from here to here , and you have accomplish the aspiration of all existence the aspiration of your consciousness which aspire to immortality to be in essence eternity itself enlightened immortal to be it eternity itself, same is the aspiration of your DNA in a journey of refinement of convergence of evolution mutation changing endless, it aspire for immortality that will be the last convergence of evolution of your DNA , the accomplishment of your DNA and consciousness that I repeat they are overlapping each other , in an eternal journey of convergence of evolution mutation changing going towards immortality eternal resurrection, going towards been in essence eternity itself , if you ask the psychologist they will tell you that all the inner search is not to know God but to be God itself is an analogy God do not exist at all is the greatest fiction opium of humanity, but it so all the inner search research is to be immortal eternal life eternal resurrection , than the triumph of civilization the triumph of life an organic unity as return at home into eternity totally enlightened , that is civilization to me , in fact a joke Donald Trump is not sleeping in the night is turning and tossing because he fear death like hell and is waiting for my report urgently all the time which is the way to immortality and eternal life , I joke smile please , but that the way it is . However let come back to the subject , religious freedom is against freedom , because basically all out of date expire fanatics religions tell only lies and lies neurosis mercy less , superstition , prejudice , illiterate ignorance , fairy tale for retarded children , that make human being conscious retarded , crippled , slave to traditions ideology bogus false dead and out of date ,blind , with inferiority complex and guilty complex , all religions are hypothetical there is no trace of what you call God is the greatest fiction of humanity , a joke when the Russian make the first flight to the moon it is say that when they were close to the moon one of the two astronauts called the central of earth in Moscow and say we are approaching the moon and there is no sign or trace of Gods or Goddesses ha ha great , there is no God is only a fiction an hypothesis never exist anywhere , another wish fulfillment of the unconscious of human being ask the psychologist they say that when you are a child you have a father then of course die and the little men fear the infinity of the universal body it fear life it fear death, and he create a mighty father in the sky as safety a protection but is infantile childish , it do not exist any God in my vision sorry enough of fairy tale for retarded children , ashamed . Anyhow in the world today they are dozens of religions big sect small sect and sect within sects , the big shot Christianity , Muslim , Jew , are monotheistic religions they have only one God hypothetical dictatorial an hypothesis that dictate your life very undemocratic , absurd , and they are multi theistic religions like the Indus where they have hundreds of Gods divinity , whole is God the sum of part of whole is God and they give names of course to their Gods , a little less dictatorial but still dictatorial hypothesis that dictate your life absolutely undemocratic dictatorial, with superstition prejudice , lies neurosis , now either the monotheistic approach of one God dictatorial is called anthropomorphism that means to give a face to a faceless reality to personalize God, to give image character, behavior , that dictate influence your life totally completely, creating a disease human being is a disease a cancer irreversible, that create multiple sclerosis, Alzheimer, and dozens of psychological neurosis , lies falsity , infantile childish , or either the multi theistic religions are anthropomorphism they give many faces to a faceless reality, and of course a wide personality because God is the sum of the total part of the universe so he has a wide personality, and many faces and of course they give many image many characters many behaviors, the multi theistic approach is really a big mess of anthropomorphism that make human being conscious retarded , disease with MS multiple sclerosis, and Alzheimer a terrible disease , and with dozens of psychological diseases , a disaster catastrophe in booth the cases of monotheistic approach or multi theistic approach , all pseudo neurosis , lies after lies hypocrisy after hypocrisy , a cancer of humanity a deep hypnosis that create unconscious asleep sleep walker , a disease human being that around forty years is life collapsed into terrible incurable psychological irreversible disease, because the unconscious build is to crystallize irreversible most of the cases . However they are also Godless religions Buddhism , Taoist , so called Zen , they look a little better from faraway , but in reality they have and they are a huge anthropomorphism too , they are very dictatorial they may have no God but they thousands of law , and absolute unconscious traditional behavior , and basically their symbology that make them absolutely anthropomorphic , they are very dictatorial undemocratic again hypothesis that dictate your life completely , no freedom , their anthropomorphism of course give image character behavior to their godless ideology, somehow they give different faces ideology to a faceless reality , maybe even more that the God oriented religions , of course the outcome is MS multiple sclerosis, Alzheimer terrible psychological diseases , dozens of neurosis , finally the anthropomorphism approach of all the religions of the world is cancer that stop any evolution opening in intelligence in consciousness formless awareness at thousands of years ago , all religions all of them castrate the human being for any further evolution mutation opening , they deprive the human being of any freedom for any inner evolution they make the human being blind , slave , illiterate ignorant , crippled , with inferiority complex and guilty complex , infantile , childish , follower of dead out date expire infantile traditions , insane , senile , so when you say religious freedom religions are against freedom they make a human being an adamant , insane senile , dementia senile , and do you want this freedom to widespread dementia senile insanity , are you crazy or something , the religions they have to harry up to give resignation by their own free will and if not they are abolish band by a new world constitution , because we want a world conscious aware and a human being healthy and whole some , religions old out of date expire they only create division split , into humanity, fearless wars for futile motivation of ideal , catastrophe, killing, destruction bloodshed , enough , they create idiom is a Greek word that means someone who live in is private dream not connected not link to any reality and the people who live in a idiom are called idiot , do you want this freedom to be adamant senile insane , with MS multiple sclerosis, Alzheimer , to live in a idiom like idiot , unconscious asleep , totally hypnotize with out of date traditions fairy tale for retarded children infantile , sleep walker , and destroy our planet earth with wars, destruction, killing bloodshed for futile motivation of division of ideal , we are sorry no more not allowed to destroy the world and killing people holy sacred divine extension of our own consciousness not allowed is a crime , not allowed anymore to widespread insanity dementia senile that make human being diseases with multiple neurosis and psychological neurosis , anthropomorphic with this cancer , we are sorry is over you please got update with the new orientation direction where the world is going headed in 2019 our contemporary age, and followed got up date in consciousness formless awareness got updated into the law of eternity, the only true authentic alternative reality , this body the consciousness awareness this planet earth the lotus paradise, for a new era to unfold of harmony , love peace , balance , celebration playfulness , freedom , compassion , meditation consciousness formless awareness , bridge link to the mystical union oneness with the law of eternity itself   sacred holy divine ….welcome   Angelo Aulisa

Angelo Aulisa

Chapter 5 Religious freedom & God fiction part two Master mode

Hi friends beloved friends , freedom from freedom for , & freedom , what is important is to define the search , basically important is to understand freedom from the unconscious ego mind , freedom from collective unconscious where is store all past culture conditioning of out of date expire dead traditions, of out of date expire religions , of expire ideology, where is store all wounds conditioning of society system , family , where basically is store all past of humanity that condition dictate your unconscious behavior completely , the collective unconscious is huge immense it goes backwards at when the first primitive barbarous men come to be , at when the first quantum leap from animals layers to humanoid to human being happen unfold , is very huge immense the collective unconscious it pierce penetrate the cosmic unconscious and all of your past life as human thousands trust me , and if you really want be accurate it penetrate pierce in a retrospective journey all of your past life layer as animals too, and all of past life layers of plants nature too and all of your past life evolution of your unconscious as rocks , where your unconscious energy was completely asleep, and of your past life journey unconscious as flowing water where your unconscious was moving unconscious intrinsic to water but flowing , than of your unconscious journey towards an evolution of unconscious when you were jut microorganism bacteria amino acid , than the irrational jump into super conscious, formless of course and dissolution into super conscious or non being body incorporeal, where time, space, forms, duality of mind completely annihilate into formless relation less unfocused awareness, that is just I am ness, infinite light infinite relaxation, dissolution diffusion into non being body incorporeal, and you were just light into the core and source of the mystery of the universal body and of life and death and of all duality of mind eternity itself, that means no begin no end oceanic light, no size infinite infinity, you in essence were jut light , as I explain in the previsions book that I write, you can do your inner journey to enlightenment from two direction inwards backwards in retrospective, all the journey into the cosmic unconscious or call it to understand more clear (spiritual body) that I call it in contemporary terminology conscious body, up to the really button of it, at when the irrational quantum leap happen into the super conscious, or non being body incorporeal, where time, space, forms ,duality of dialectics of opposite complementary completely ceases annihilate , or you can do the journey in the opposite direction upwards higher, through meditation refining more and more your light consciousness from unconscious , until really the ultimate stage of light consciousness emptiness nothingness, when your light consciousness turn up on itself, because no more relation of subject or object all as annihilate at the event of the overlapping non being body incorporeal, where whole annihilate time, space, forms duality of mind, and dialectics , and the witnessing consciousness having no more relation of any kind annihilate, twisted into formless relation less unfocused awareness, rising higher and higher, awareness that is just I am ness, infinite light, infinite relaxation into the core and source of the mystery of the universal body and of life and death and of all duality of mind and dialectics of opposite complementary, eternity itself meaning no begin no end oceanic light, no size just an open relativity an infinite opening not absolute at all begin less and endless , and then enlightenment happen unfold, your essence merge mingled annihilate into the oceanic light of eternity, in a journey upwards done factual scientific through meditation up and up higher and higher , so either you go deeper and deeper inwards through the cosmic unconscious, inner journey to enlightenment, or either you go higher and higher upwards through the inner journey of meditation and enlightenment happen unfold, you in essence reach the same source core of eternity itself, that is oceanic light no begin or end , no size infinity, and what remain is just a pillar of light consciousness within you, in booth the inner journey either retrospective deeper and deeper through the unconscious, or either the inner journey of meditation gradual of higher and higher upwards through refining your consciousness , what remain finally is a pillar of light consciousness within you ,no more dark unconscious, because booth the journey the request is that your witness consciousness should be awake, and the witnessing of all the journey inner deeper or higher upwards of meditation will burn of all of your past life of all layers, the cosmos will reabsorb them , conditioning wounds of unconscious, and free completely your unconscious , what remain is a pillar of light consciousness, an inner bliss sacred holy emptiness nothingness, silence peace rich with intrinsic subtle ecstasy zest, free flowing in light consciousness and you in essence are enlightened forever and ever, guaranty they never give guaranty but if you do this inner journey that I describe in accuracy enlightenment will be yours forever and ever guaranty . However freedom from unconscious individual from collective unconscious, from unconscious asleep, from various hypnosis, of religions expire out of date from traditions dead expire out of date, from ideology system society , family conditioning expire out of date , is what is all about freedom from unconscious ego mind , here I describe the two direction orientation that you can journey, however they are allot of therapy that help you to clean up free your unconscious , meditation and witness consciousness is very effective , they are dynamic meditation to clean up the unconscious, gibberish meditation to help to clean up your ego mind from parental voice, society voice as television voice computer voice that are an in print conditioning into your ego mind , the objective is to clean up and free your neurons that have been feed projected with conditioning wounds, repression, falsity lies neurosis, the neurons should return clean empty fresh, you know that the neurons function in chain reaction into your brain vector of thought emotion believe, and those information make up your life, basically the in print into the neurons is what the unconscious his , we have to work up on it with various therapy to clean up free up your neurons, and consequence your unconscious ego mind got free clean fresh , you may say but this is brain wash , yes , your mind is dirty it stink , you never take a shower a bath since many many life it need to be clean wash take a shower of witness consciousness to be again free clean , so that universal consciousness can be the contents of your neurons, and consequence your neurons become vector of universal light consciousness into your brain in a chain reaction, and be vector of dharma quality intrinsic to consciousness such as love , intelligence , bliss sacred holy divine, silence peace intrinsic with subtle ecstasy zest , freedom the very essence of consciousness , playfulness , celebration , affirmation of life and all of is sacred aspect faces in freedom , so that your brain become the divine sacred holy consciousness workshop , the old out of date expire false religions say that an empty brain is the evil workshop , the other way around is the truth, a loaded brain of unconscious wounds conditioning staff is the evil workshop, that by the way do not exist any evil what is evil, is your repression conditioning wounds of unconscious staff, that is what the superstition expire religions call evil your unconscious saturated with conditioning wounds repression, and some time it stem up in pent up of unconscious , and an empty brain is the divine sacred holy workshop of the fundamental law intrinsic to the universal body consciousness, that is pulsation of love pulsation of intelligence pulsation of light wave pulsation of dharma quality such as bliss sacred holy such as silence peace with intrinsic subtle ecstasy zest pulsation of freedom pulsation of naturalness spontaneity pulsation of innocence pulsation of playfulness , pulsation of celebration life the very fabric of life , a pulsation of creativity that as never ever stop pulsating since the big bang onwards at when consciousness come into light into existing in relation of the universal body itself , and so then your neurons free and clean become vector of what they were supposed to be vector of holiness sacredness consciousness, of quality of love and intelligence pure and innocent, naturalness, spontaneity, freedom . The religions out of date and expire they have play a very dirty vicious game , of conditioning of falsity, lies neurosis, superstition prejudice , old religions are against life, against freedom, against spontaneity, against naturalness, against celebration, against playfulness, against affirmation of life, against sciences and physics ashamed, against woman ashamed they do not think that woman have a soul really ashamed half population of the world is woman , they are against natural spontaneous sexual behavior an intrinsic quality essence nature of human being, they are for celibacy that is a crime against humanity that create monster priest pedophilia, and dozens of sexual perversion into human being you cannot repress the sexual river energy of a human being is a crime against humanity with dramatic consequence , religions old and out of date make you dull and dead crippled conscious retarded , old expire religions are the cancer of humanity, very vicious and deadly , I say this thing because the harm that old out of date expire religions are doing to humanity is countless, they are destroying planet earth with division of ideal ideology, with fearless wars, destruction, bloodshed, catastrophe killing butchering of human kind , a crime against humanity perpetuate since millennia , they divide split the organic unity from his own inner being witness consciousness and inner consciousness formless awareness , standing in between men and consciousness, fake priest as false mediators they split human being from the inner source of consciousness awareness from the core and source of eternity itself ,creating division of sacred and profane, when the reality is indivisible is a oneness mystical union indivisible, your body is the visible soul and your inner being is the invisible soul in mystical union indivisible , the priest create division so they can stand on a higher plane then you, they are spiritual and they can condemn you, and you are just profane a sinner, this is the most vicious game ever play on humanity and human being, it as to finish right now, the other way around the truth they are sinner preacher of lies, hypocrisy, neurosis, falsity superstition, prejudice, absurdity fairy tale for retarded children, and you human being are innocent pure without any pretension of spirituality but simple alive , I repeat there is no division of inner and outer of sacred and profane but is all one reality mystical union indivisible, the inner is the outer and outer is the inner overlapping each other extension of one another , and if you want really know the profane the life is sacred holy, and the sacred of the so called priest is profane because is all a preaching of lies falsity, hypocrisy, neurosis, superstition, prejudice that make human being conscious retarded, crippled with inferiority complex, and guilty complex, insane adamant senile, this is a crime against humanity that as to finish right now is not allowed to widespread such an insanity , to make human being slave with tradition blind is a crime against humanity, enough give resignation right now to all religions , there is no division inner and outer are one reality, like life and death are one reality, two faces of a single coin, one is life the other face is death, and the coin itself is the eternal consciousness awareness eternity itself , in fact the synthesis of life thesis and death antithesis friction of those and synthesis of eternal life, the coin itself, no division at all is one mystical union indivisible inner and outer , death is the fruit that grows on trees of life intrinsic part of life , religions old out of date expire have done such an harm to human being in such an ugly terrible way, with lies, falsity, hypocrisy, conditioning, repression that is time to give up resignation for them right now . However then freedom for a new dawn of civilization, intelligence , consciousness formless awareness, for the entire universal body one consciousness empty of contents labels adjectives no interpretation of the little unconscious men can define consciousness, to infinite to enclose in labels adjectives contents, consciousness it belong to itself is nobody monopoly , neutral to gender, color, race age , anyone can be in mystical union oneness with consciousness, the path the way meditation, silence love , painting , dancing , singing , playing music , running tennis any activity that take you in essence into the present moment, into no mind into your inner being is meditation, any activity that do not interfere psychological and do not interfere physically with other human being is meditation, link, bridge through your inner being (soul) from the known to the unknown of universal consciousness, and be one in mystical union with it in bliss in silence, in peace with intrinsic subtle ecstasy zest , and the journey is an eternal journey, the forms the body die but your consciousness formless awareness are immortal eternal already resurrected, the resurrection is a subtle mysterious alchemy conscious alchemy not gross not physical not material, but a conscious subtle mysterious alchemy from unconscious to light empty consciousness, to formless awareness to the core and source of eternity itself, that is begin less endless oceanic light , freedom for civilization ultimate stage of civilization where weapons are a crime against humanity, is a huge big crime to kill an extension of your own consciousness a living being sacred holy divine, so the device of death called weapons are a crime against humanity , into intrinsic to consciousness we are an oceanic mystical union oneness extension of one another, into the objectivity 8 billion of forms body , freedom for an ultimate stage of civilization where the wars are a crime against humanity and to build weapons the factory that those this production are a crime against humanity, they should change their production into beneficial item for humanity like equipment to reduce pollution, clean ear clean water rivers oceans , that is very much needed for the world and humanity such an equipment to reduce climate change for a better life of quality clean no pollution , if we give all the resource that are going for death and destruction like weapons wars military , to physics sciences they can restore the echo system and climate change, even if it look like an impossible task change but sciences physics have an immense power , freedom for a world of a new era of harmony, peace, love freedom, respect of human right, balance between nations keep by intelligence consciousness awareness compassion, and not the one who has the most horrible weapons is the strongest, that is the law of the jungle the gorilla behave that way finish abolish band, a new era of a world conscious aware is always the only answer alternative , and is urgent this new dawn of meditation consciousness awareness , is a razor edge between the old men little men unconscious, the out of date expire religions, traditions out of date expire ,ideology out of date expire, that they have all the power in their hands to destroy planets earth they are unconscious asleep, hypnotize, sleep walker very dangerous situation , and the enlightened one the awakened one that they sheer light into the world consciousness awareness, is a race , my proposal let come together in understanding is fundamental, and let actualize the dream of civilization that human kind is dreaming since ten thousand years, but never as happen it as remain a beautiful talking dream , let give up the ugly heritage traditions of wars of the past ancient humanity , is an ugly heritage that the new man meditative conscious aware do not want, we got better things to do then wars, destruction ,killing, bloodshed , we got to celebrate life affirm life, love the mystery miracle that life his sacred holy divine, we are not the ancient primitive men barbarous unconscious, that fight wars blind unconscious we refuse such heritage , freedom for this body the consciousness awareness this planet earth the lotus paradise , the first step abolish wars weapons military as a crime against humanity, then the ultimate stage of civilization can begin unfold a new era of love, celebration, playfulness, meditation, consciousness, awareness , because this human being on earth of today as never experience what it means to live a Zen dimension a meditative dimension, is all another plane of living trust, the Zen dimension is just & freedom, sensitive plus, loving plus, mystical union oneness plus, with the universal consciousness with the organism of the universal body, and with the core and source of eternity itself, is completely another plane of living another level where you do not need alcohol , drugs , medicine opioid , bullshit like that, but what you need is to go deep in meditation and consciousness is a universal alchemy in itself, that you are always in bliss, not in happiness that as the opposite complementary in sadness and just behind the corner sadness is waiting to jump on you , no bliss as no opposite complementary is forever one ecstasy zest is enlightenment ever , sensitiveness that just to be alive purposeless is the greatest miracle, when your eyes meet the greenery of the nature, the color of the flower, the blue of the sky, and the singing birds are a divine music sacred holy divine, and then you are in wonder breathless in enlightenment one in mystical union with core and source of eternity, ha this the ha experience describe by the psychologist ha this thousand time ha this in wonder at the miracle mystery that life his, in love with the mystery miracle that life his for no purpose at all just been alive enlightened , is so mysterious intriguing ha this yes thousand time ha this welcome Angelo Aulisa ...

Angelo Aulisa

Chapter 6 The seven astral body of mysticism Master mode

Hi friends beloved friends , we are going to do an inner journey into one of the most true authentic methodology of mysticism , a human being organic unity is much more than matter material , body , we are something very subtle mysterious , transcendental above beyond of material physical form , basically inner being witness consciousness, universal consciousness, formless awareness , an organic unity clean of ego mind unconscious which is a huge task in essence is eternity itself begin less endless , immortal , enlightened , already resurrected into the present life that you live . However an organic unity has different stage subtle layers into is body , an organic unity has seven layer of different plane level of living , that in this methodology are called astral body seven different level stage intrinsic to our organic unity in a subtle mysterious way , I am going to explain to you the different astral body that are our full prospect reality of our body life , so the first body is called physical body the second etheric body the third astral body the forth mental body the fifth conscious body or for your understanding (spiritual body) the six is the cosmic body the seventh is non being body incorporeal ,one very important insight of this methodology is the dialectics law of opposite complementary of the astral body , if you are a woman into the physical body you are man at the etheric body and woman at the astral body and man at the mental body, into the conscious body (spiritual body) gender are transcended the conscious body is neutral the cosmic body is neutral non being body is formless beyond the law of dialectics into non being body incorporeal the law of dialectics and forms are completely annihilate transcended , so a woman is man at the stage of mental body is better that she seek enlightenment through is astral body the unconscious where she is woman more receptive , and man at a stage of mental body is woman he can seek enlightenment through is mental body because is woman there and is more receptive, I have already explain this methodology through all my books many time very accurate if you look through all my 17 books you will find this methodology of the seven astral body chapter on it many time , because to me the seven astral body is really the fifth essence of mysticism , very important true methodology scientific methodology factual methodology for your day to day life , the seven astral body is not something esoteric far out is a methodology very accurate of the inner mystery reality of an organic unity it describe the all rainbow prospect potential of our inner journey into meditation, inner being witness consciousness , universal consciousness , nothingness emptiness, non being body incorporeal formless awareness that is just an I am ness infinite light infinite relaxation into the core and source of the mystery of the universal body and of life and death and of all duality of mind and dialectics , eternity itself no begin no end the meaning of eternity that is oceanic light , no size eternity is an open relativity not absolute at all an opening into infinity , is infinite freedom from all and everything , time space , forms duality of mind and dialectics , the real freedom infinite bliss , peace silence , were enlightenment happen unfold , we are going to do an inner journey with the methodology of the seven astral body piercing penetrating our organic unity within up to the very core and source of eternity , they are different stage level in this inner journey to go through and we are going through all the phases of the eternal inner journey . Anyhow the first body is the physical body most of humanity knows and live at a plane stage of physical body only the material dimension most of humanity knows only matter 99 per cent of humanity live into the surface of objectivity and knows only the matter the physical body is a superficial dimension of having more and more of matter material very ordinary linear logics is the horizontal dimension of ego mind unconscious which goes in a linear horizontal logic on the surface of objectivity from abc to xvz , at infinite regression gazing starring at the horizon tomorrow is gone be the happiness the love the loving approach not today not now they live projected into an imaginary future that never come, the ego mind unconscious knows how to look only outwards categorically it never ever look inwards within , as not such a quality of looking within and the ego unconscious mind as no quality of love or loving , love it do not belong to the mind ego , if the ego is present love is absent if the ego is absent love is present , however the physical body live and move on the surface of the objectivity it move in time if is ten am and you go to your office you will reach to the office at 10.15 am , it move on time , than we got the etheric body , that is the emotional layer of your organic unity emotion are elusive one minute are there next minute are gone they pass by they have more roots then thoughts but they are anyhow elusive , the etheric body move on space but the time remain the same , for example if you are here talking with me but you are thinking of your beloved in new York you are not here with me you have move your emotional layer in new York at your beloved , the time remain the same 10 am here 10 am in new York , when you move your emotional layer somewhere else you are where you put your attention all the time so you are not here with me only your body is here with me , the etheric body can move on space the time remain the same you can move wherever you want like just put the attention where you intend to go , then we got the astral body which is your individual unconscious and collective unconscious , you can move into your unconscious in retrospective backwards at the primal scream when you born , and further you can move in retrospective into the collective unconscious backwards up to the really button of it is huge infinite , to journey into the unconscious is very important so then you can witness with your witness consciousness all the conditioning repression , wounds , trauma , that you have going through all your life and the witness consciousness is the fire that burn of all conditioning wounds repression trauma of your unconscious the observation is the medicine that evaporate the unconscious the cosmos reabsorb all conditioning wounds repression staff of your unconscious either collective either individual unconscious and clean up frees your unconscious , they are no tablets or chemical medicine for healing your unconscious for cleaning frees your unconscious your witness consciousness is the only medicine that those this dirty job , to journey into the unconscious in retrospective is an healing reviews mode very necessary is safety measure that is inbuilt natural into your organic unity , then we got the mental body into the mental body you can move forwards into the imaginary future and backwards into the past into the factual memory of your mind but one at the time , the mental body is very huge immense we know only 10 per cent of our brain 90 per cent of our brain is unknown and it hide infinite potential unknown to us , they are many ways to stimulate the brain many substance to stimulate the brain , but basically we know very little of our magnificent organ called brain , they are people who have stimulate their brain a little more than other and they stumble on telepathy , chiaro vegency the prediction of the future , revelation of the future , reading thought of other , this are all characteristic coming from the unknown part of the brain , and many other esoteric power all of them are coming from our unknown part of the brain , you know the most intelligence average of genius knows use is brain at 12 per cent , the ordinary average is 7 per cent ordinary people use their brain only seven per cent , and our brain as capacity that allowed in only 2 per cent of the total information hear , the 98 per cent as a natural capacity quality to expel them this is nice because most of the information are useless , now when you journey forwards into the mental body you are stimulating your imagination because the future as yet to come is imaginative , but imagination can be a good quality to develop intuition even if objective superficial intuition , but anyhow imagination is a good quality tool , and when you are moving backwards you are moving into a dead tense , into your factual memory which is different from the insight of the unconscious the factual memory is more superficial of thought of past ordinary remembrance you have to be carefully to not mistake factual memory with the insight of the unconscious which are more deep heavy conditioning wounds , however the mental body is huge immense little is known of it the brain remain a mystery for 90 per cent of is function , for instance an enlightened one can use is brain much more than an ordinary men , almost hundred per cent , but this is a note in the chapter , the size of the first 4 astral body remain the physical size same size of your physical size always , however than we got the conscious body (spiritual body) here happen a quantum leap an irrational jump a convergence of evolution from the horizontal dimension of body mind ego unconscious to the vertical dimension of your inner being of deeper and higher , the present moment , is the gate less gate to the vertical dimension of your inner being into the conscious body (spiritual body) you got centered into your inner being and witness consciousness , you let your light consciousness flowing deeper within your organic unity into your inner being the process is trigger by the so called dark matter or gravitational energy field that pull bend your light consciousness deeper into your inner being at the deepest point of your inner being , once you are centered into your inner being simultaneous you are centered into the whole existence and you will realize that you are a crystal clear witness consciousness , not your body not your thought not your emotion not even your senses but a crystal clear witness consciousness got centered into your inner being and witness consciousness , into the conscious body or (spiritual body) that goes in retrospective in a journey into the all cosmic unconscious up the very source and core of super conscious or non being body incorporeal where time space , forms duality of mind and of dialectics completely annihilate , you can move with your witness consciousness awake up the very button end of it up to the super conscious in a journey of digital color of many layer of the cosmic unconscious you will pierce penetrate the first layer that is all of your past life thousands and see it in digital color I remind you that the journey unfold backwards not forwards and this is important to determinate if the journey is real a journey into your cosmic unconscious past life it unfold backwards , then you will pierce the layer of the past life of animals you have being many kind of animals and you can witness it , then you will pierce the layer of nature trees plant a vortex of color unfold at this stage majestic you are immerse into a vortex of color , then you will pierce the layer of rocks when you unconscious energy evolving was completely asleep , then the layer of water flowing unconscious intrinsic to water then the layer of microorganism bacteria amino acid the break of life then the irrational jump quantum leap into the super conscious non being body incorporeal where forms time space duality whole annihilate and you in essence will be diffuse annihilate into infinite oceanic light white and transparent mingled merge into it , the inner journey as end you have return in retrospective journey in a circle of zero into the oceanic light of eternity itself , if you ever return into the body you will be enlightened forever and ever if you do not return into the body than an eternal resurrection has happen unfold, formless you will be have an universal body a new begin intrinsic to universal consciousness and all forms and living being of the universal body , the conscious body or (spiritual body) the size remain the same as physical body up to the quantum leap into the super conscious then of course no size infinity , is a majestic inner journey the first revelation if you ever return into the body from the journey is that death do not exist you have witness thousands of past life you were you are you will be , and that is very important to live a relax life you will know by experience the fiction of death , however once that you are centered deep into your inner being and you are just a crystal clear witness consciousness and a mirror like quality a moment come that only pin drop silence is there nothing more to witness and the pin drop silence is the gate less gate to the next body the cosmic body , here happen another quantum leap convergence of evolution your inner being and witness consciousness will turn up on itself having no more subject or object relation to witness they will turn up on itself and annihilate twisted into universal consciousness and witnessing consciousness the witnessing of the universal body itself is a break through majestic the size change into universal size you in essence will be huge as the universal body is big infinite you in essence will be intrinsic to the universal body and all of is forms intrinsic to universal consciousness one in mystical union with it , is divine sacred holy inner experience you in essence in light consciousness will start move rising higher and higher at the event horizon of the universal body this pulling up this rising higher is trigger by the so called dark energy or expansive energy field that pull upwards higher and higher at the event horizon of the universal body and you will expand in synchronicity with it on and on , at this stage you are the universal body itself your inner being is the inner being of whole universal body is a sacred majestic break through , and on and on your light consciousness will flow move circulate into the universal body this movement flowing circulation of your light empty consciousness is trigger by the so called dark flux or flowing energy field that moves flows planets galaxies stars in and out of the universal body into the overlapping non being body incorporeal where time space forms duality of mind and dialectics annihilate and the flowing energy field will move circulate flows your light empty consciousness too in and out of the universal body that is overlapping with non being body incorporeal like a universal breath in and out , than emptiness nothingness are the gate less gate to non being body incorporeal , here at this stage the witnessing consciousness of the universal body will turn up on itself and annihilate completely because the consciousness is always in relation to a subject or object up to the event of non being body the relation of consciousness was the universal body itself but here at this stage of annihilating into non being body the universal body is no more and the consciousness turn up on itself and annihilate twisted into formless relation less unfocused awareness that is just an I am ness infinite light infinite relaxation , awareness ultimate essence of the core and source of eternity itself that is transcendental above beyond life and death is just eternal life without any opposite complementary , also in life is a continuous of being conscious when there is subject or object and then when there is no subject or object just no mind you are just aware relax relation less is a shift of conscious and aware all the time when you are aware you are totally relax into core and source of eternity itself silence peace bliss relaxation ha this just empty of thought emotion just freedom , this the methodology of the seven astral body so that you know all the time where you are, one should be always in the present in the moment flowing moment to moment here now centered into his own inner being witness consciousness into his own mirror like quality into is inner consciousness flowing into formless awareness always one in mystical union one with the core and source of eternity itself one should be in essence eternity itself , enlightened awake ,in bliss in freedom into enlightenment, this methodology show you the path of the inner journey of meditation and show you where you really are all the time   if you are just a physical body or if you are moving into your emotion the etheric body or if you are unconscious into the astral body journeying into the unconscious or if you are just moving into the mental body past factual memory or future imagination or if you are journey into the cosmic unconscious and witness past life or if you are into universal consciousness into the universal body conscious or if you are just aware relax relation less diffuse annihilate into the core and source of eternity itself, is like a GPS of your inner mystery reality of your organic unity you will know always where you are dwelling , certain the witness consciousness should be awake , you see the process of meditation you can called a process of annihilation of your inner essence up to the very core and source of eternity itself then the annihilation finish end, than you in essence will be eternity itself enlightened forever and ever you will be within just a pillar of light and oceanic light enlightened , all the seven astral body finally annihilate into the core and source of the mystery of the universal body and of life and death and of all duality of mind and dialectics , eternity itself meaning no begin no end oceanic light , and you in essence will be eternity

itself eternal immortal enlightened forever and ever , awake from unconscious asleep and various hypnosis , you will be just enlightenment just light within and without forever and ever …..Welcome
Angelo Aulisa

Angelo Aulisa

Chapter 7 The higher mathematics of mysticism Master mode

Hi friends beloved friends , ordinary into the world exist a lower mathematics where two plus two is 4 , and that the way it is mathematics is not an opinion but a factual science a fact , the ordinary human being see himself just like a little small unconscious dot into the universe , he is just a small dot and the universal body is huge immense infinite and the little unconscious men feel himself just a dot meaningless , and that the way it is in an ordinary objective material dimension of matter the dimension of having , the horizontal dimension of the ego mind unconscious linear logic on the surface of objectivity superficial , he is just matter no soul , no consciousness , no awareness , just a machine a robot , no love just a loveless insignificant life a machine robot , the little unconscious men live on the surface of life on the objectivity in an horizontal dimension with an Aristotelian logic of rational association of thought with a double fold logic yes or no black or white linear from abc to xvz at infinite regression because gazing starring outwards at the horizon you live projected into an imaginary future that as yet to come nobody knows if it will be or not , existence as no obligation to fulfill your imagination your dream so gazing at the horizon the horizon recede backwards and remain always elusive at horizon , the ego mind unconscious as no quality capacity to look within it look always outwards at the other at the horizon and life remain always a dream elusive the distance of the horizon remain always the same until death come one day , the little unconscious men is just a machine a robot he is not an organism , he eat food is transformed in energy he is a compulsion of chain reaction of eating food transforming food in energy that give him limited energy to live the life , until death when he die trembling unconscious he as live a meaningless life in vane , material on the dimension of having horizontal of eating drinking and be marry life as pass in a split second and now is the time to die unconscious trembling an time as run out , to live a life unconscious your death is gone be unconscious too and it will generate reincarnation soon you will be reborn and have other opportunity to become conscious aware of the inner mystery reality of an organic unity , what create an organic unity the organic unity is create into the dimension of being inner being into the vertical dimension , the moment the present is the gate less of the vertical dimension of deeper and higher of your inner being , you close your eyes bring the attention within and let your light consciousness flow deeper and deeper into your inner being this inner alchemy of going deeper into your inner being is trigger by the so called dark matter or gravitational energy field that pull bent your light consciousness deeper at the center of your inner being where you will realize that you are not your body not your thoughts process not your emotion process not your unconscious staff of conditioning wounds not even your senses but you are a crystal clear witness consciousness a mirror like quality , once you are centered into your inner being when nothing more remain to witness at the deepest point of your inner being pin drop silence is the gate less gate to your inner universal consciousness where your inner being and witness consciousness annihilate into the universal body is a break through you in essence will be one intrinsic the universal body and the universal consciousness and the witnessing consciousness of the universal body itself , your light consciousness will start rise higher and higher expanding at infinite this process of rising higher and higher expanding is trigger by the so called dark energy of expansive energy field that is expanding our universe every split second on and on and your light consciousness to will expand rise higher in synchronicity with the expansion of the universal body , and your light consciousness will move flow circulate into the universal body and in and out of the universal body into the overlapping non being body incorporeal like a universal breath , the universal body breath , in and out , is majestic sacred holy divine, this process of breathing of the universe is trigger by the so called dark flux that moves flows circulate planets galaxies stars into the universal body in an irrational play, way and in and out of the universal body into non being body incorporeal where forms time space duality of mind and dialectics completely annihilate and he will moves flows circulate also your light consciousness in the same way in and out of the universal body into the overlapping non being body incorporeal , here at this stage your inner being is the whole universal body you in essence are intrinsic to all forms and living being of the universal body in mystical union oneness , and here your body turn twisted into an organic unity become an organic unity in mystical union with the organism of the universal body one indivisible intrinsic one , that from where come from the term organic unity of the organism of the universal body consciousness confer organism to your organic unity body holy sacred divine , and your energy will be unlimited you will have infinite energy , you will be one in mystical union with the source and core of unconditional love and intelligence your intelligence will be intelligence of the whole universal body and your love will be the love of the whole universal body , you will be an extension of pulsation of love pulsation of intelligence pulsation of light waves pulsation of dharma quality such as bliss sacred holy divine such as peace silence rich with intrinsic subtle ecstasy zest , a pulsation of freedom essence the very ground of consciousness , a pulsation of creativity that as never stop pulsating since the big bang onwards when consciousness come into be into light as a fundamental law intrinsic into the universal body , in relation of the universal body , your inner being will be the link the bridge extension that connected your organic unity to consciousness from the unknown in this case to the known of your inner being and your inner being will extend consciousness to your hearth to your emotional layer and your hearth will extend consciousness to your neurons into your brain your brain will become the divine sacred holy workshop of consciousness , and your brain finally will extend your consciousness outwards into the objectivity of the world into your life , and only then you are an organic unity before then you are simple matter a robot a machine an unconscious ego mind , the difference is immense infinite the machine robot is not really alive is dead , sorry I am sorry but this is the truth , hence the saying of Jesus let the dead burry their own dead very strong , only an organic unity is really alive the organism of the universal body and universal consciousness confer organism aliveness to the organic unity , however let come back on the overlapping of the universal body and non being body incorporeal than nothingness emptiness are the gate less gate to non being body incorporeal where time space duality of mind and dialectics and forms annihilate completely and the empty light witnessing consciousness turn up on itself and annihilate too no more relation of subject or object for consciousness so it annihilate too it turn twisted into formless relation less unfocused awareness that is just an I am ness infinite light infinite relaxation , awareness ultimate essence into the core and source of the mystery of the universal body and of life and death and of all duality of mind and dialectics , eternity itself no begin no end the meaning oceanic light no size it vanish into infinity like the ultimate equation of quantum mathematics infinity and no more equation follow , it vanish into an open relativity not absolute at all no begin no end just an infinite opening , it vanish into infinite freedom from all and everything forms duality time space the real freedom infinite bliss silence peace ecstasy . Here at home enlightenment unfold happen immortality unfold is realize the resurrection has happen already , mind you the resurrection is a conscious alchemy not gross not material not physical but a subtle mysterious alchemy conscious alchemy from unconscious to light consciousness to formless awareness to eternity itself where your essence quality fragrance data of intelligence that you have refine in thousands of life your DNA in short will annihilate dissolve diffuse into the oceanic light of eternity itself, into awareness into a new begin you will have be intrinsic in essence formless into the universal body and universal consciousness and intrinsic into the all forms and living being of the universal body , into enlightenment you will be oceanic light forever and ever and eternity to come that the resurrection meaning is an endless eternal journey that end nowhere ever . However let come back to the subject of higher mathematics now , the little unconscious men looking at the infinite universe he think that the universe is huge immense and I am small a dot true in ordinary mathematics , but as you got centered into your inner being another mathematics come into be that the infinite universe exist because I exist if I ceases to exist also the universe ceases to exist we exist into an interdependence mutual , so we are equal I am and the universe his so we are equal , true authentic , you start feel equal to the universe you are part intrinsic of the universe and the universe his part intrinsic of you , a mystical union a oneness happen , basically because when you got centered into your inner being simultaneous you in essence are centered into the whole existence your inner being (soul) is the link bridge from the known to the unknown of universal consciousness formless awareness the core and source of eternity itself , the alchemy unfold natural spontaneous afford less , so you start feel equal to the universal body and that is true authentic beautiful you feel huge immense transcendental a break through majestic sacred holy divine , than on an on elaborating a new convergence of evolution happen unfold looking at the universal body you start to realize that you are conscious of the organism of universal body you are conscious aware of it, instead the universal body is blissful unconscious , enchanting beautiful the universal body but blissful unconscious and you are conscious aware of it here happen a tremendous beautiful convergence of evolution quantum leap you in essence in consciousness formless awareness enlightened are bigger huger than the universal body itself because you conscious aware of it and the universal body is blissful unconscious your consciousness awareness your enlightenment , make you in essence bigger huger than the universe itself , and that the way it is a great break through has happen unfold your inner consciousness awareness your enlightenment make of you sacred holy divine expression of eternity even bigger huger than the universal body itself , the fundamental law intrinsic to the universal body consciousness itself is like a thread running through the all forms and living being of the universal body but you have to got, be in mystical union in oneness with it our inner being (soul) trigger this mystical union oneness this organism , religion to me means organism literally and inner being means integration the soul is what integrate you in essence into an organism into an organic unity , the human being is the most refine expression of the whole universal body I would say the most important expression form of the whole existence because he can become conscious of himself conscious of the whole universal body conscious aware of the core and source of the mystery of the universal body and of life and death and of all duality of mind and dialectics eternity itself , no begin no end infinite oceanic light no size , he can be eternity itself he can be it intrinsic one, clean of unconscious ego mind of course , no other form expression of eternity can be that do that is a privilege of the human being the most refine expression of whole existence , hence bigger huger even of the universal body itself blissful unconscious , through is consciousness awareness through is enlightenment …. That the higher mathematics of mysticism true and real .welcome Angelo Aulisa

Angelo Aulisa

Chapter 8 The law of dialectics of mysticism Master mode

Hi friends beloved friends , we are going to explain clear in this chapter one of the most important law of the core and source of the mystery of the universal body and of life and death and of all duality of mind and dialectics , eternity itself no begin no end meaning oceanic light eternity as no size the size vanish into infinity into an open relativity not absolute at all no begin no end just an opening infinite , infinite freedom infinite bliss sacred holy divine infinite silence peace ecstasy eternal life beyond duality of dialectics immortality core and source of resurrection ,   that what eternity means his , the dialectics law of opposite complementary is the law of nature is the fundamental law intrinsic to eternity not to the universal body but to eternity it transcend goes beyond above even of the universal body ,the law of dialectics is intrinsic at the primordial silence, emptiness nothingness before of the big bang event billions of years before the law of dialectics of nature was already intrinsic to primordial silence emptiness nothingness absence of things the law of dialectics of nature of opposite complementary is a scientific methodology like there is quantum mathematics that is a scientific methodology that I respect completely so there is a methodology called the law of dialectics of opposite complementary like thesis , antithesis , friction and synthesis that at is on turn it twisted into a thesis again and again antithesis again friction and a new synthesis unfold and so on so forth at infinity , you have to go on make this equation of thesis , antithesis friction and synthesis until the very end button of the methodology , in the universal body in the world whole and everything as is complementary opposite is all a duality of opposite complementary , man thesis woman antithesis friction and synthesis of love a life can be generate by such a synthesis , day and night synthesis timeless , life and death synthesis eternal life , love and heath synthesis compassion love plus passion , hanger and satiety synthesis relaxation wellbeing , activity and passivity synthesis meditation Zen , relaxation peace stillness , and so on so forth in the nature of the world all is a duality of opposite complementary , for instance even our language talking is a thesis and antithesis and synthesis you understand what one is meaning talking about only because of is opposite complementary , example I love you understand because of heath what he means by love , life you understand in contrast of death what he means , day you understand the language because of night and so on so forth language is dual in relation of his opposite complementary you can talk and understand what one means , basically in whole planets earth and in the entire universal body is all a friction of thesis and antithesis and synthesis is all a game play of duality dialectics of duality that in the surface they look contradictory but deep down they exist in mutual oneness mystical union , woman exist because of men otherwise if men was not existing how you understand that one is a woman day exist because of night otherwise how you could understand that the day exist because exist the night , death exist because of life otherwise how you could understand what death his only because exist life and so on so forth they are mutual interdependent in mystical union, one exist because of the other , and in the world and the universe is whole a play game of opposite complementary on the surface they look contradictory but deep down in reality they complement each other in mutual interdependence ,and so the law of nature the law of dialectics come into be contemporary to the primordial emptiness nothingness silence of whole existence , how for the simple fact that emptiness and nothingness silence exist in relation to emptiness nothingness absence of things silence the law of nature of dialectics come into be into existing , all the existence it generate self-generate by alchemy play of intrinsic law forces energy in motion intrinsic to whole existence eternity itself , for example at begin less begin was absolute emptiness nothingness absence of things pin drop silence this simple fact generate intrinsic the law of dialectics of opposite complementary as a consequence of the existing of emptiness nothingness silence , because thesis micro, emptiness nothingness silence, have create the opposite complementary antithesis of soundless sound for silence opposite and macro wholeness fullness for nothingness emptiness friction of those and synthesis of the core and source of eternity itself oceanic light whiteness and transparent no begin no end it generate at the primordial ages by this synthesis that i describe here , and eternity is eternal life beyond transcendental to any opposite complementary you would say why because death and destruction are the opposite complementary of eternal life but then again emptiness nothingness pin drop silence that at the apex of singularity create a antithesis of soundless sound of AUM a vibration intrinsic to existence itself of macro of wholeness fullness and friction and synthesis of the core and source of eternity oceanic light no size infinity again and again at infinitum eternity is the end of o duality of dialectics is indestructible it recreate itself again and again at infinite , I repeat the all existence it generate is self-generate by a play of alchemy of intrinsic law forces energy in motion intrinsic within to the all existence certain an irrational play of opposite complementary that on the surface they look contradictory that why irrational but deep down are complementary mutual interdependent they complement each other they complete each other , for example a man alone is half a woman alone is half they are opposite complementary together they complement they complete each other into an whole total, the circle of zero turn complete alone they are an half circle unless one is enlightened , but that is just a note , however here the law of eternity and how it self-generate itself I remind you that at this stage age we are in the primordial phases of existence itself where the big bang as yet to happen, the big bang is distant billions of years yet ,we are on the phases of the core and source of eternity itself no begin no end oceanic light no size the size vanish into an open relativity not absolute at all because no begin no end just an infinite opening sacred holy divine , and we are in the sleeping age of the universe the universal body as yet to be generate no big bang yet , this phase probable lost billions of years , of emptiness nothingness silence, infinite light oceanic light intrinsic of course to the law of eternity , objectivity on the surface was absolute darkness void emptiness nothingness frozen cold 270 degrees below zero , in billions of years was create the situation circumstance the momentum, of absolute emptiness nothingness that at the apex of it of infinitesimal of micro of nothingness emptiness a singularity was create micro smaller infinitesimal then an atoms thesis , that at his own turn create an antithesis of macro wholeness fullness , friction of those and synthesis of big bang a great explosion come into light that was 14 billion and 300 million years ago , the event of big bang generate simultaneous the coming into light of whole the intrinsic law forces energy in motion intrinsic into the universal body ,time and space was generate we count our time and space from the event of big bang onwards before was no time no space but just timeless infinity , simultaneous the inflection of the explosion that is even on today expanding somehow our universe , simultaneous the Boson x was generate that is the quality that keep together the all universal body and confer Massa to particles strings atoms matter , and cannot be otherwise because the cloud immense huge of dust gas debris that the big bang generate was huger then galaxies of today , and the Massa of particles strings atoms matter that compose the compound of gas dust debris was confer to it by the Boson x itself , otherwise no Massa of matter was possible , so simultaneous come into light the Boson x itself that confer Massa matter to whole and everything into the universal body , simultaneous I remind you always simultaneous in relation of the universal body itself the fundamental law of consciousness come to be in light intrinsic to the universal body , consciousness is a fundamental inner law of the universal body that need always and always a relation of subject or object to be in this case the relation is the whole universal body and consciousness will go on to be until when after billions of years the universal body itself will annihilate disappear vanish disintegrated due the pulling up higher apart of the dark energy or expansive energy field that is expanding our universal body at incredible speed and in billions of years it will annihilate disintegrate it , consciousness will exist and be until that day , after having no more relation of subject or object will turn up on itself and annihilate , however consciousness confer organism to the universal body consciousness is the inner fabric of life of the universal body is subtle mysterious sacred holy divine play, creativity, quality intrinsic to the universal body consciousness is a pulsation of love a pulsation of intelligence a pulsation of light waves a pulsation of dharma quality Dharma means intrinsic sacred holy quality such as bliss sacred holy divine such as silence peace with intrinsic subtle ecstasy zest , consciousness is a pulsation of naturalness spontaneity innocence, a pulsation of freedom the very ground essence of consciousness a pulsation of creativity that as never stop pulsating a split second since the big bang event at when it come to be into light , consciousness confer organism oneness togetherness holiness sacredness unite in mystical union the whole universal body is like an inner thread that runs through intrinsic into the whole forms and living being of the universal body , a fundamental inner law of the universal body it belong to itself is nobody monopoly, as no labels no adjectives no contents is just an empty light waves of consciousness and is neutral to gender color race ages , neutral to any partial interpretation of the little unconscious men , consciousness is everywhere and nowhere in particular intrinsic to the universal body and anyone can be in mystical union oneness with consciousness the path the way the link that connected you to universal consciousness is meditation , silence love , painting , dancing , singing , playing music , tennis running or any activity that take you in essence into moment into the present into no mind into your inner being in short is meditation that link connected you in essence to universal consciousness the link the bridge is your inner being (soul) that is the bridge from the known to the unknown of universal consciousness and consciousness is the link the bridge that connected link you to the unknowable of infinity of the core and source of eternity itself , however the Boson x is a fundamental law quality intrinsic to the universal body that confer Massa to particles strings atoms matter a law alchemy in itself same it belong to nobody it belong to itself is nobody monopoly , and the fundamental intrinsic law of consciousness is a law in itself that confer organism holiness sacredness put together unite into an organism the whole universal body , they come to be simultaneous at the big bang event , however simultaneous at the big bang event the inner law of dark matter or gravitational energy field come to be in light intrinsic to the universal body , the gravitational energy field is a gravitation expand into the universal body everywhere and nowhere in particular it assemble together with is gravitational pull planets stars galaxies , is the great painter of the universal body , the only explanation we have how galaxies stays together so enchanting is the gravitational pull of dark matter of the gravitational energy field , it influences the whole universal body planet earth the all forms and living being of the universal body and human being too , it take a share of 24 per cent of the universal body , is a powerful gravitational energy field expand everywhere into the universal body it come to be simultaneous at the big bang time , in fact after the big bang we have 3 billion years of dark ages of the universal body where it was the huge cloud of dust gas debris thanks to the dark matter gravitational energy field it took 3 billion years to see assembled the first stars planets , those 3 billion years when it was nothing just the huge cloud is called by the physicist the dark ages of the universal body , the universal body that you see today so beautiful enchanting is the work of assembling together of planets stars galaxies of the gravitational energy field the great painter of the universal body , that pull together unite it pull deeper , however simultaneous at the big bang event another fundamental law intrinsic to the universal body come to be in light intrinsic , the so called dark energy or expansive energy field , that pull higher up , it pull apart expand the universe , physicist until 30 years ago they were thinking that our universe was static , with the evolution of physics they discover that our universe is expanding at incredible speed due the pulling higher up a part of the dark energy or expansive energy field , that if it goes on expanding our universe so speed in billions of years will disintegrate completely our universal body , if you were there after billions of years you will look up to the sky and no planets no stars no galaxies anymore whole disintegrate by the pulling of the expansive energy field it would be just cold frozen void darkness emptiness nothingness our universal body vanish disintegrate , anyhow don't panic because at this stage when the apex of infinitesimal of emptiness nothingness come to is crescendo momentum again the micro singularity smaller than an atoms and again the antithesis of macro wholeness fullness and again a friction and again a synthesis of new big bang for a law of dialectics that is the most important inner intrinsic law of whole existence the law of nature of opposite complementary , and again and again a new universal body will be create , we are not the first universal body and this universal body will be no the last one is an eternal cycle of universal body they was other universal body before ours they will be other after , what is important is that you in essence take shelter into the law of eternity that is huger bigger beyond above transcendental to whole universal body that will come into be into light , eternity as no begin or end eternity is the ultimate canvas reality where all the mysterious sacred holy show of all cycle of all universal body are paint display , you in essence intrinsic one into eternity will be witnessing all cycle of universes that will come to be , anyhow the dark energy or expansive energy field take a share of the universal body of 72 per cent , the reason why the dark energy as not yet disintegrate our universal body is because is a perfect complementary opposite antithesis of the dark matter or gravitational energy field that create a perfect antithesis, friction and a synthesis of harmony balance that somehow keep our universal body together , but for how long not so long because the difference of share of this two intrinsic law is to huge one is 72 per cent the other 24 per cent so the gravitational energy field dark matter can hold for a while the disintegration but in the long run the dark energy will win the race and will tell a part our universal body ,however simultaneous at the big bang event another fundamental law intrinsic to the universal body come to be the dark flux or flowing energy field that is an intrinsic force energy in motion into the universal body that moves flows circulate all our universal body in an irrational play it moves planets stars galaxies in an irrational play into our universal body and it moves them at event of horizon of our universal body where they disappear into non being body incorporeal where time space forms duality of mind and dialectics completely annihilate non being body is overlapping with the universal body is huger bigger above beyond transcendental of the universal body ultimate canvas reality where our universal body mysterious sacred holy divine show is paint display as no size is infinite infinity an open relativity not absolute at all just an infinite opening no begin or end , and then mysteriously they reappear into our universal body like an universal breath in and out of the universal body , however the fundamental law of dialectics of nature is the master key to unfold the major mystery of the inner mystery reality of an organic unity that a human being his and the master key to unfold the major mystery of the universal body and eternity itself , the law of nature of dialectics of opposite complementary as always exist intrinsic to existence itself previsions to the big bang event , and all of this play of intrinsic law forces energy in motion into eternity itself and into the universal body itself is an eternal play alchemy self-generate certain subtle mysterious a mystery what is mystery is that as no cause what has no cause create a mystery, what as a cause create a cause and effect , the mystery remain intact but that is the beauty what make life fresh unknown each second an exploration, but we can know and live intrinsic within one in mystical union with the mystery of the universal body and of life and death and of all duality of mind and dialectics eternity itself, no begin no end oceanic light no size infinity , we can be one in mystical union enlightened intrinsic to the oceanic light of eternity in enlightenment, immortal death do not exist is just the greatest fiction of humanity the form body die but our consciousness awareness is an eternal journey that end nowhere endless , that is it the strings factuality reality true authentic of mysticism welcome Angelo Aulisa

Angelo Aulisa

Chapter 9 Consciousness & awareness nuance & difference Master mode

Hi friends beloved friends, in this chapter we are going to highlight consciousness to highlight awareness and describe the differences nuance between the two, because many time I hear say we must bring awareness to this matter or subject or object not possible is a wrong assertion expression you can bring consciousness to this matter or subject or object , because consciousness is always in relation to some matter or object or subject you can bring consciousness not awareness because awareness is always categorically relation less formless unfocused just an I am ness, infinite light, infinite relaxation , awareness is the ultimate essence into the core and source of the mystery of the universal body and life and death and of all duality of mind and dialectics , eternity itself meaning no begin no end , oceanic light no size infinity, the size it vanish into an open relativity not absolute at all because it has no begin or end is an opening infinite , eternity is the end of dialectics of opposite complementary, into eternity only a oneness a suchness eternal life eternal bliss eternal, freedom from whole and everything time, space duality of mind and dialectics the real freedom , peace silence rich with intrinsic subtle ecstasy zest ,eternity is the core and source of unconditional love and unconditional intelligence , into eternity reside unfold all the essence quality fragrance data of intelligence that one refine in thousands of life our DNA refine in short of all the enlightened one, who have gone for an eternal resurrection here at home you can be in mystical union one with the masters that you have loved that you love, the master key the bridge that connected link you to the beloved one is your love for them, and you can have a meeting a merging of consciousness formless awareness a mystical union a oneness with the beloved one masters that you love, and drink from his wisdom from is essence quality feel it the essence of intelligence of the masters that you love , have sacred holy date with the divine beloved masters that you love and have a confirmation that death is really a great fiction it do not exist and have a confirmation that the eternal resurrection is a true authentic reality through your own experience of meeting in silence in meditation in Zen your beloved one of your hearth the masters that you love ,is a majestic divine experience experimentation that is hard to transfer in words is simple majestic subtle mysterious sacred holy divine ,mind you the resurrection is a conscious alchemy not physical not gross not material but a subtle mysterious conscious alchemy, from unconscious to inner being to witness consciousness to universal consciousness to emptiness nothingness gate less gate to non being body incorporeal where forms duality of mind and dialectics and space and time completely annihilate, into relation less formless unfocused awareness, that is just an I am ness infinite light infinite relaxation , awareness ultimate essence of the core and source of the mystery of the universal body and of life and death and of duality of mind and dialectics , eternity itself no begin no end no size, infinity, the size vanish into an open relativity not absolute at all just a sacred holy divine opening infinite , where your essence quality fragrance data of intelligence that you refine in thousands of life your DNA refine in short annihilate dissolve diffuse into the core and source of eternity , that what means resurrection a new begin with an universal body into intrinsic to universal consciousness that is a fundamental law intrinsic to the universal body like an inner thread that runs through intrinsic to all forms and living being of the universal body, and you will be flowing intrinsic to it for eternity to come as core and source of it . Once in my life I did one hundred session of Zen meditation focusing on meeting all the beloved masters that I have loved in my life, meeting how in essence in quality in consciousness in awareness that year the place where I did the session was flooded the river that cross the town overflows , it was a divine enchanting experience of deep meditation, I repeat the master key is your love the bridge is your love and then the sky will shower down on you like rain of flowers and you will be flooded , but basically I did this experience to see which of those master was authentic real intrinsic to the universal body and universal consciousness, many they were a great confirmation of the eternal life eternal resurrection happen , not that I needed prove I do not need any prove was just a search of how many masters where connected link in love with me many they were , so strong unbelievable unsayable very subtle mysterious experience of Zen meditation, certain you must be in tuning in that time I was meditating since dozen of years I was I am also now just consciousness awareness, a deep experience acquaintance in Zen in meditation is require to do such an experience . However let go deep into the subject of this chapter the only way is this, be in the moment in the present gate less gate to your inner reality mystery of your organic unity, close your eyes and let your light consciousness flow deeper into your inner being the so called dark matter or gravitational energy field will pull bend your light consciousness deep at the center of your inner being, this because gravity bend time and space and gravity bend light consciousness too this alchemy of flowing your light consciousness deeper into your inner being is trigger by the gravitational energy field called dark matter, dark stand for unknowing do not got scare but today days we know much more than you think about it , however when you are centered deep into your inner being relaxed into it you will realize that you are not your body, not your thought process not your emotion process, not your unconscious conditioning wounds staff, not even your senses but you are a crystal clear witness consciousness a mirror like quality , deeper in meditation a moment come where there is nothing to witness anymore it take time years but this is the process of annihilation of meditation , than pin drop silence is the gate less gate to your inner universal consciousness, here happen a break through your inner being and witness consciousness will annihilate into the universal body and universal consciousness and witnessing consciousness of the whole universal body, is majestic divine sacred holy you in essence are intrinsic one in mystical union with the whole universal body and consciousness, your consciousness will start to rise higher and higher expanding everywhere and nowhere in particular intrinsic to whole universal body and forms living being of it, rising higher the process of expansion ,rising higher is trigger by the so called dark energy or expansive energy field that will rise higher your inner light consciousness at the horizon event of the universal body, expanding in synchronicity with it , at this stage your inner being is the whole universal body and you are huger and big as the whole universal body your size is the size of the whole universal body. you in essence are intrinsic into it , expanding higher and higher at infinite is majestic sacred holy, a bliss that surpass all understanding , on and on in Zen mediation your light consciousness flows moves circulate in an irrational play intrinsic to the universal body this flowing of your light empty consciousness is trigger by the so called dark flux or flowing energy field, that is a force an energy in motion into intrinsic to the universal body that move flows circulate planets stars galaxies in an irrational play into the universal body, and in & out at the horizon event of the universal body, into the overlapping non being body incorporeal where time space duality of mind and dialectics completely annihilate, they disappear annihilate into it, stars planets galaxies like an universal breath in and out, and suddenly they reappear into the universal body , in the same way the flowing energy field will move in and out of the universal body your light empty consciousness into non being body incorporeal, which is overlapping with the universal body, on and on of this process of breathing of the universe emptiness nothingness the gate less gate to nonbeing body incorporeal, where I repeat time space forms duality of mind , dialectics completely annihilate, your light consciousness witnessing consciousness will turn up on itself and annihilate too, because consciousness is always and always in relation to a subject or object, in this stage particular consciousness was in relation to the subject of whole universal body, entering non being body incorporeal where all annihilate, consciousness simple ceases to be it turn twisted into formless unfocused relation less awareness, that is just an I am ness infinite light infinite relaxation , now I want say that in our day to day life they are plenty of moment like this where you are conscious of a subject or object a situation circumstance but suddenly all subject or object situation circumstance drop ceases and your consciousness shift into formless awareness relation less awareness, unfocused awareness, moment of silence gap of silence where there is no subject or object, those are the moment where your consciousness relapsed into awareness into the core and source of the mystery of the universe and of life and death and of all duality of mind and dialectics into eternity itself , relax let go into this tremendous relaxation into the core and source of eternity, fearless those are the moment when you recharge your battery , the core and source of eternity as tremendous healing power it will rejuvenate you refresh you regenerate you , give moment to your life where you are just thought less emotion less a no mind in silence those gap of silence are mediation Zen, where you are one in mystical union with the core and source of eternity itself and are moment of awareness , than shift again into consciousness in being conscious of something or other subject or object , than again shift into awareness , this is the basic difference of consciousness and awareness , consciousness is always regarding in relation of a subject or object lower somehow, instead awareness is relation less unfocused formless higher somehow, no forms into the core and source of non being eternity itself, just an I am ness infinite light cool light whiteness transparency moon like , infinite relaxation, where into source and core of eternity itself you recharge you refresh rejuvenate regenerate your inner being your organic unity , actually your brain is an mentasm working 24 hours per day in the day is in thoughts dreaming process all day, in the night it dream thousands and one dream , give a rest to your brain, the moment of silence the moment where all subject object drop and they are gap of no mind are moment of Zen mediation, moment of awareness let go into it easy fearless do not got scare of silence emptiness nothingness absence of things object or subject, are moment where the gate less gate into awareness open up and you refresh regenerate rejuvenate for real, you cannot even imagine the healing power of the core and source of eternity, the blessing the relaxation ha this , many time during the day you got moment like this of silence, been conscious, and shift into relation less of object or subject , those are the gap moment of awareness let go into it and enjoy rejoice is a luxury you are just an I am ness , infinite light , an awareness ultimate essence of the core and source of the mystery of the universal body and of life and death and of all duality of mind and dialectics , eternity itself meaning no begin no end oceanic light no size just infinity, infinite freedom the real freedom , you in essence are at home into eternity where enlightenment happen where immortality unfold happen reside, where the resurrection has already happen into your living body life, where you are awake from unconscious asleep and various hypnosis where you are just an oceanic light enlightened in bliss, that is not happiness that has the opposite complementary into sadness just behind the corner , but bliss no opposite complementary forever and ever enlightened , and you will never feel lonely because basic this are the two fear of human kind death and be lonely, at home into the core of eternity you will be alone divide the word into two all one in mystical union oneness with the core and source of eternity itself, where reside in essence quality fragrance data of intelligence that you refine in thousands of life the DNA in short completely refine, of all enlightened one who have had an eternal resurrection , the immortality the resurrection eternal is not a joke but a true reality authentic real hundred per cent , you will be in great company all the time try to think Gautama the Buddha will be there Jesus will be there Mahavira will be there Osho will be there Lao-tzu and thousands of enlightened masters, and most of all universal body and forms and living being of it will be one in mystical union with you in essence, you will be all one with the whole existence and lonely missing the other will be laughing stock , basically you will be enlightened in bliss in freedom forever and ever , that is it bring consciousness to this subject of this chapter not awareness is not possible here explain the nuance difference of consciousness and awareness ... very useful for your day to day life factual reality. Welcome Angelo Aulisa

Angelo Aulisa

Chapter 10 The new dawn of civilization consciousness awareness Master mode

Hi friends beloved friends , in this chapter we are going to highlight the most important points of the new dawn of civilization, intelligence, meditation, consciousness, formless awareness, into the core and source of the mystery of the universal body and of life and death, duality of mind , dialectics , eternity itself meaning no begin no end , oceanic light , no size infinity the size of eternity vanish into an open relativity not absolute at all just an infinite opening , eternity is huger bigger above beyond , transcendental than the universal body itself, actually ultimate canvas reality where the mysterious holy sacred divine show of the universal body is display paint , eternity is beyond, transcendental to dialectics of opposite complementary into eternity all duality ceases, is just a oneness a suchness eternal life without opposite complementary , eternity is infinite freedom from whole and everything time , space , forms , duality of mind and dialectics, the real freedom , infinite bliss sacred holy divine , infinite silence peace rich within intrinsic subtle ecstasy zest eternity is source and core of unconditional love, unconditional intelligence , a miracle of playfulness celebration affirmation of life in all of is faces aspects , eternity is core and source of naturalness spontaneity innocence , into eternity you in essence are at home where enlightenment happen unfold forever and ever, where immortality is realize happen where resurrection happen unfold , the resurrection is a conscious alchemy not gross not physical not material but a subtle mysterious alchemy conscious, from unconscious to inner being to witness consciousness, to universal consciousness, to nothingness emptiness gate less gate to non being body incorporeal where time, space , forms , duality of mind and dialectics completely annihilate, and the universal consciousness too annihilate because consciousness is always in relation to a subject or object into non being body incorporeal whole and everything annihilate nothing survive ,and consciousness turn up on itself annihilate , turn twisted into formless relation less unfocused awareness, that is just an I am ness, infinite light, infinite relaxation bliss , awareness ultimate essence of the core and source of the mystery of the universal body, of life and death, of all duality of mind , dialectics eternity itself no begin no end , oceanic light no size just infinity , where one day when you leave your body your essence, fragrance, quality, data of intelligence that you refine in thousands of life your DNA annihilate, dissolve diffuse into, for an eternal resurrection , a new begin intrinsic one with eternity. into formless awareness, into with an universal body, intrinsic to universal consciousness fundamental law intrinsic into the universal body, that is like a thread that runs through all forms and living being of the universal body , in essence you will be flowing eternally for eternity to come that the meaning of resurrection a conscious subtle mysterious alchemy , and an organic unity in essence clean of unconscious ego mind is eternity itself one intrinsic it , immortal , resurrected already in the present living life , enlightened awake forever, from unconscious asleep and various hypnosis ,the world this human kind need urgent a new dawn of consciousness fundamental intrinsic law of the universal body, that is a pulsation of love a pulsation of intelligence, a pulsation of light waves, a pulsation of dharma quality such as bliss sacred holy divine, silence peace rich with intrinsic ecstasy zest , a pulsation of freedom the very essence ground of consciousness, a pulsation of naturalness spontaneity innocence, a pulsation of playfulness celebration, a pulsation of creativity that as never for a split second stop pulsating since the big bang onwards when it come into be in relation of the universal body itself , consciousness is an alchemy in itself it belong to nobody is nobody monopoly , consciousness is label less contents less adjective less neutral to any interpretation of part of the little unconscious men, consciousness cannot be enclosed into an adjective label to huge big infinite , consciousness is neutral to gender ages color races , anybody can be in mystical union one intrinsic to consciousness, the path the way meditation ZEN silence , love , dancing , singing , painting , playing music , sculpting , running tennis , or any activity that do not interfere with psychological freedom of others, do not interfere in the physical body of other organic unity, that take you in essence into the present moment, into no mind into your inner being in short is meditation, link bridge that connected you in essence in mystical union with universal consciousness, your inner being is the bridge link from the known to the unknown of universal consciousness that connected you in mystical sacred holy union oneness with consciousness, and consciousness is the bridge link that connected you in essence from the unknown of consciousness to the unknowable of the core and source of eternity itself in oneness in sacred holy bless , the world human kind need urgent to get understand this true authentic knowledge and widespread this new authentic inner science of mysticism & physics , the world of the future will be guided for 90 per cent from physics sciences, and 10 per cent from mysticism the inner science of the inner mystery reality of an organic unity , and physics means the knowledge of nature the knowledge of the universal body behavior, the goal of physics is to understand how the universe behave, and how the intrinsic law forces energy in motion into the universal body behave and finally define them know them , this two science that are opposite complementary turn into a unique synthesis of a unique science that surpass all understand of human kind up to now , a mystical revolution is under way that will transform the objectivity surface of planet earth in a way that you cannot even image, and will transform the inner reality mystery of an organic unity in a way that you have not even dream about ,in the next hundred years humanity will have a convergence of evolution quantum leap into consciousness awareness that will transform this planet into the lotus paradise and our organic unity into consciousness awareness, one in mystical union with the core and source of eternity , no begin no end oceanic light infinity , we will have a humanity of enlightened being, enlightenment will be the new era age of humanity , all and everybody enlightened , will be a new era of harmony balance, of intelligence of consciousness, formless awareness, of love peace, playfulness celebration , of creativity , of quality bliss, of naturalness spontaneity innocence , a new dawn of ultimate civilization , where weapons are abolish as a crime against humanity, whereas consequence wars are abolish as a crime against humanity, military are abolish, they will do beneficial works function for humanity peaceful , where factory industry of weapons are abolish as a crime against humanity, transformed in beneficial item for humanity like equipment to reduce pollution, climate change, clean ear, clean rivers oceans , a clean echo system , this task challenge will be taken over by physics and sciences that with all resources economic coming from the stoppage of wars destruction killing bloodshed , that are a huge income of resources, will try to stop climate change an various pollution into the world today, only sciences can do this miracle of changing climate change and restore the echo system , and with the resource coming from the abolishment of weapons wars military we will restore the poverty starvation of the world where is needed urgent , and of course build a new world natural biological at measure of the new men conscious aware meditative , we will abolish all of the out of date expire superstition false religions all of them as a crime against humanity, perpetuate since millennia , no more allowed to widespread insanity dementia senile lies neurosis falsity , fairy tale for retarded children that make the human being crippled, conscious retarded, with inferiority complex guilty complex unsort pathologic , with dozens of psychological disease neurosis, like MS multiple sclerosis and Alzheimer terrible disease the cause of those diseases are the old out of date expire religions, so they will be all of them abolish band from a new world constitution one for the all world , an further all the nations of the world they will be abolish as they are conceive today, no rigid border no rigid nations but functional nations with functional government like post office, all unite one in harmony balance by a strong unite nation govern, with a single world constitution for the entire world , society and system they will be totally transform no more rigid family, human kind will be unite by a single inner thread of love that in truth is the very essence inner ground of our inner being, a human being in essence into is (soul) inner being is love itself, and love will be the inner thread that unite all of us in togetherness in oneness in love , a relation will lost until love is there than we are 8 billion we will change, different relation more universality of love , the children we will be all uncles , they will grow more free with an universal mind more fathers more mothers which they will be less possessive less attached, and consequence the child will grow in freedom universality and love , certain we need to open millions of mystery school university of mysticism all over the world, where people will have the opportunity to meditate become conscious aware one in mystical union with universal consciousness and with the core and source of eternity itself, meaning no begin no end oceanic light no size, just infinite infinity just an open relativity not absolute at all but just an infinite opening into eternity boundless , the opening of mystery school and university of mysticism is fundamental important to transform the theory the knowledge of mysticism & physics into a real authentic experience, because finally only the experience will transform your inner being your inner world of mystery and reality , the theory is not enough you need a real experience lived deep of meditation of mystery school university of mysticism which they will be microcosms of people from all over the world seeking enlightenment, learning meditation Zen , living together eating, meditating, dancing, celebrating the miracle of life together in love in playfulness of all kind, painting playing music singing, sculpting and all art generally and all creativity generally, celebrating affirming life in all of his sacred holy aspect, they will be academy of life center of life where the theory will be transformed in real experience, because finally only the experience will change transform you within your inner being and without , and basically into the mystery school university of mysticism you will understand learn that the family is over is a small unity of few people that hinder the freedom life in all the sense, you shrink into the family you get a shrink vision of life window less, freedom less very limited, the family is a small unity of few people a part from the world you get a narrow shrink vision , into the academy of life mystery school university of mysticism you will experience the universality opening of life, you expand you get an universal vision a universal approach to life in freedom in love in meditation Zen , finally you will experience what it means to live a meditative sensitive dimension of Zen meditation, all another plane level of living life full of zest sensitiveness full of juice of love full of juice of togetherness , with all living being enlightened awakened one, and with the all universal body universal consciousness in organism in mystical union oneness, you will see the life for the first time how real his supposed to be lived in consciousness formless awareness, intrinsic one with the core and source of eternity itself, wow a mystical revolution the world will live a new era for real of real life love peace, ultimate stage of civilization harmony balance , wow this the dream of a new humanity a celebrative affirmative humanity , where love is the inner thread that unite us all , love the very essence of our soul inner being love you are it , Jesus use to say God is love I use to say love is God because God do not exist is the greatest fiction falsity opium of humanity, so love our very inner nature essence of our inner being soul that extended into the objectivity, unite us all in an cosmic orgasm of joy celebration playfulness .That is it, this short beautiful book end here Master mode is the greatest book ever write in the history of human kind, hope you have enjoy the inner journey and that this book help you all to be more conscious aware, to live a better life of quality of essence, and brings to you a convergence of evolution of DNA in intelligence an opening into the organism of the universal body, an opening into the core and source of eternity itself, and of course a mystical union oneness in essence with it , my proposal forever and ever a new dawn of civilization, of meditation, of consciousness, awareness urgent needed by the world the only alternative true and authentic, and the only answer is always a world conscious aware meditative , I want finish like this God is dead and now Zen is the only living truth, this planet the lotus paradise, this body the very consciousness awareness , I elevate the human being to the highest possibility potentiality of being enlightened living in enlightenment, awake from unconscious asleep and various hypnosis, conscious aware the human being is God as analogy God do not exist , and the God of ancient out of date religions is really dead I hope so, again God is dead and now Zen is the only living truth true authentic real ... welcome love all of you thank you Angelo Aulisa